NEW BIRTH

Pathway to the Kingdom of God

Eva Peck

© 2018 by Eva Peck
All rights reserved
Except for any fair dealing permitted under the Copyright Act, no part of this book may be reproduced by any means without prior permission of the author and publisher.

Foreword: Rev. Dr. Michael Nedbal

Cover and page xv graphic: Claudia Balasoiu (www.freeimages.com)
Cover design: Eva and Alex Peck
Author photo: Jindrich (Henry) Degen, edited by Alex Peck

Bible quotes, unless otherwise indicated, are taken from the *Holy Bible, New International Version.* Copyright © 1973, 1978, 1984 by International Bible Society. Used by permission of Zondervan Publishing House. All rights reserved.

ISBN: 978-0-9876279-1-9

> A catalogue record for this book is available from the National Library of Australia

The book can be purchased online through
http://www.pathway-publishing.org.
Also available at Amazon, Ingram, and other outlets worldwide.

Dedicated to
our Loving Heavenly Father
and all His children.

Other Books by the Same Author

Divine Reflections in Times and Seasons
Divine Reflections in Natural Phenomena
Divine Reflections in Living Things
Divine Insights from Human Life
Jesus' Gospel of God's Love
The Greatest Love
Salvation
Abundant Living on Small Income

Co-author of:
Pathway to Life – Through the Holy Scriptures
Journey to the Divine Within – Through Silence, Stillness and Simplicity

See also:
http://universal-spirituality.net/home-2/free-publications
and http://www.pathway-publishing.org/

Acknowledgements

First, I would like to thank the Great God, our heavenly Father, as well as our spirit guides and teachers for enabling, inspiring, and blessing this book.

I wish to thank my dear husband Alex for his unfailing love and ever-present help and support.

I also wish to thank my friends in the Divine Love community for their support and prayers, as expressed through the Divine Love Sanctuary Foundation forum, where book chapters were first published – especially Al and Jeanne Fike, Jane Gartshore, Catherine Kent, Marga McCrady, David Reed, and Steven Scott.

In addition to the Bible and transmission of inspired information by James Padgett and Daniel Samuels, I need to acknowledge drawing on the Greek expertise and insights of Rev. Mark Kramer and Anastasios Kioulachoglou. I have also drawn inspiration from a small book by the late Rev. Kenneth E. Hagin, entitled *The New Birth;* a contemporary message received by Rev. Dr. David Lampron; and an unpublished book by Bill Frase. (See Specific References in the back of the book)

Last, but not least, I am indebted to Rev. Dr. Michael Nedbal, Trustee of the Foundation Church of Divine Truth and personal friend, for carefully reviewing my manuscript and providing helpful input.

Without the help and support of these dear souls, this book would not have become what it is. So heartfelt thanks to all.

Contents

Foreword ix

Preface xi

Introduction 1

Part I – The Calling 6

Chapter 1: Soul Awakening, New Heart, and Repentance . 8

Part II – Justification 18

Chapter 2 – Two Means to Justification 23

Chapter 3 - Our Status as True Children of God 42

Chapter 4 – Possessors of Life and Immortality 59

Chapter 5 – Anointed by God 66

Chapter 6 – Transformed into a New Being 71

Chapter 7 – Change of Desires and Growth in Virtues ... 80

Chapter 8 – Transformed by Love to Love 84

Chapter 9 – Growth in Spiritual Understanding 90

Chapter 10 – Born of Water and the Spirit 94

Chapter 11 – Saved by Grace through Faith 100

Part III – Entering Divine Glory 113

Chapter 12 – Celestial Kingdom of God 114

Prayers for Divine Love 128

Epilogue.. 134

References 137

About the Author 139

About Pathway Publishing 141

Foreword

I have a high degree of respect and admiration for Rev. Eva Peck. In the years that I have known her, she has demonstrated a remarkable insight into the Holy Scriptures. Her ability to understand and communicate, in plain English, the teachings of the Bible is simply amazing – a gift from God. Eva's personal life is no less remarkable. She treats others with dignity and respect, and is a true example of walking, speaking, and acting in grace.

I have enjoyed reading many of Eva's publications. The *New Birth – Pathway to the Kingdom of God*, however, is my favorite because it is the first of its kind to illuminate the truths contained in the Bible by cross-referencing biblical texts with material from the *True Gospel Revealed Anew by Jesus* – a collection of messages received from Celestial angels and others in the spirit realms in the early 1900s. I have dedicated my life to the study of God's truths and know of no one better than Eva to bridge the gap between these two remarkable sources of spiritual information.

In her book, Eva walks us through the stages of spiritual progression beginning with soul awakening, via soul transformation, and ending with the soul becoming at-one with our heavenly Father and living in God's Celestial Kingdom. She even provides us with insights and glimpses,

Foreword

based on accounts of those now there, of what life and work might be like for the divine angels in the Kingdom of God.

I hope that you enjoy the book as much as I did. It is a remarkable journey of soul transformation validated by the Holy Scriptures.

Rev. Michael Nedbal, PhD
November, 2017

Preface

The book, *New Birth – Pathway to the Kingdom of God* proposes answers, as I presently see them, to questions many wonder about such as, what is the purpose of life and the human potential, and what, if anything, happens after this life.

Most Christians believe that man is by nature sinful – following the rebellion/fall of Adam and Eve. According to traditional teachings, this condition can be remedied by accepting Jesus Christ as a personal savior and his sacrifice on the cross as payment for our sins. This is said to reconcile us to God and cleanse us from all sin. The Bible, in the New Testament, indeed contains the teaching that man is saved by the death and blood of Jesus. While churches also usually teach that those who in this life have not accepted Jesus as their savior will eternally suffer in an ever-burning hell, the Scriptures are not quite as explicit – though they do speak about judgment.

Besides numerous passages speaking about being saved by the vicarious atonement of Jesus – his shedding of blood and dying on a Roman cross, there is also another thread or "gospel" running through the New Testament. It emphasises more of *what Jesus taught and exhorted his followers to do*, than what he did for them through his sacrificial death. Many passages speak about the Holy Spirit as the agent of transformation and creating the "new heart" predicted by Old Testament prophets. Jesus spoke about "New Birth" as a means of salvation and condition for entering the Kingdom of God. Other passages speak about Love of God shed abroad to our hearts by the Holy Spirit. We are to follow the leading of the Spirit in order to be saved. God is more than happy to give us the Holy Spirit, but our effort and cooperation are also needed in working out our own salvation.

This book focuses on what is the New Birth, how we can be born again, what it means in this life, and what we can look forward to in the next life and in the Kingdom of God that Jesus so often spoke about when he came to the earth.

It is a well-established fact (though not accepted by all Christians) that the Bible is not a book wherein every word is inspired by God. It is not a book of science or history as such. It also combines multiple threads of thought from various ancient sources. It has gone through a complex process of document selection, compilation, editing and reediting, as well as translating – all this long after the time of Jesus and the original apostles. There is no doubt that the Bible is an inspired book which has changed countless lives over the span of its existence, and that it contains the essential message of salvation. However, it is not free from errors, interpolations, extrapolations, and biases of its contributors, editors, and translators who were all influenced by the time and culture they lived in.

Preface

Several years ago, I was led to another revelation – not as well known, but, I believe, worth considering. It is a collection of inspired/mediated writings received by an American medium, James Padgett, about one hundred years ago. When I began reading these messages, they made sense. My rule of thumb for discerning truth is how it resonates with me and my experiences – regardless of what the source is or who said it. I believe that inspired truth can be found in all the main religions and many other spiritual writings. It is important to realize that all inspired knowledge is mediated knowledge – it comes from a higher source beyond us through a human spiritual teacher (who in that process functions as a medium) to be passed onto others.

In this book, I am mostly drawing on information from two sources: the four volumes of *True Gospel Revealed Anew by Jesus* (TGRABJ) published by the Foundation Church of the New Birth, and the Bible. The majority of biblical quotes are from the New International Version. The TGRABJ references include the *volume and the starting page* of the message, for example, a quote/paraphrase from TGRABJ/2/23 comes from Volume 2 and a message starting on page 23. Another related source drawn on is *New Testament Revelations* – a collection of messages received by Dr. Daniel Samuels largely in the 1950s and 60s. They are annotated as NTR, followed by the number of the revelation.

Preface

The author hopes and prays that readers will, with an open mind, consider the presented views and decide whether what they read resonates with them. May they be inspired and encouraged, as well as motivated to act on what they learn, so that they can start on the journey of fulfilling their unlimited human potential.

Eva Peck
November 2017

The gist of this book is the New Birth or birth from above, which means a new heart or a transformed soul through God's Divine Love. Butterflies are a fitting symbol of transformation – from an earth-bound ordinary creature to a limitless glorious being of indescribable beauty.

Introduction

One day while speaking with Nicodemus, Jesus pointed out that to gain entrance into the Kingdom of God, one must be *born again* or *born from above*. He compared and contrasted the natural human birth with the "birth of water and the spirit."

John 3:3-8 – Jesus answered and said to [Nicodemus], "Most assuredly, I say to you, unless one is born again [the Greek literally says 'born from above' – see also NIV margin], he cannot see the kingdom of God." Nicodemus said to him, "How can a man be born when he is old? Can he enter a second time into his mother's womb and be born?" Jesus answered, "Most assuredly, I say to you, unless one is born of water and the Spirit, he cannot enter the kingdom of God. That which is born of the flesh is flesh, and that which is born of the Spirit is spirit. Do not marvel that I said to you, 'You must be born again.' The wind blows where it wishes, and you hear the sound of it, but cannot tell where it comes from and where it goes. So is everyone who is born of the Spirit."

Indeed, the physical birth can serve as an analogy – though imperfect as all analogies are – of the spiritual birth. Here are some insights.

Before we are born as humans, we go through three stages: Firstly, *conception* when the short-lived female ovum is fertilized by the male sperm, giving it a much greater potential and longer life than it would have of and by itself. Secondly, there is a period of *gestation or development*, during which the embryo undergoes a remarkable transformation into a tiny human being with the characteristics of its parents. Thirdly, the actual *birth* takes place, through which the baby enters the physical world. (In the original Greek, there is just one word, *genao*, which apparently can mean both begettal / conception and birth.)

The "new birth" or "birth from above" also can be seen as having three stages, summed up in Romans 8:

Romans 8:29-30 – For those God foreknew he also predestined to be conformed to the likeness of his Son, that he might be the firstborn among many brothers. And those he predestined, he also *called*; those he called, he also *justified*; those he justified, he also *glorified*.

From the above passage, the New Birth of the Spirit can be equated with being conformed into the likeness of Jesus, or becoming a son or daughter of God in the same way that Jesus has. He is the firstborn or pioneer of our salvation, with many to follow in his steps. The process very broadly consists of a calling, justification and glorification.

Theologian John Wesley also conceptualized grace – the process of salvation – into three types or phases. He called them *prevenient grace, justifying grace*, and *sanctifying grace*.

Introduction

Below is a brief summary of each of the three phases which, with their sub-phases, are discussed in more detail in the chapters of the book.

The Calling – In this first step, the soul is opened or awakened through the Divine Love, and the person becomes receptive and enabled to follow the way to salvation. This is analogous to conception.

In John Wesley's concept of prevenient grace, God's grace stirs up within us a desire to know our heavenly Father and empowers us to respond to His invitation – the calling – to a relationship with God. Wesley understood grace as God's active presence in our lives. This presence is not dependent on human actions or response. It is a gift that is always available, but that can be refused. God takes the initiative in relating to humanity. We do not have to beg and plead for God's love and grace. God actively seeks us and wants all to be saved (1 Timothy 2:4). Because of being given freedom to choose, not all will, however, accept this most gracious offer.

Justification – Secondly, we are *justified* or in Paul's words to the church in Corinth: "In Christ, God was *reconciling the world to himself, not counting their trespasses against them*" (2 Corinthians 5:19). There is reconciliation, pardon and restoration of relationship with God. According to John Wesley, the image of God — which has been distorted by sin — is renewed within us through God's grace.

Introduction

As we shall see later, there is actually more to it than just renewing a distorted image. But again, this dimension of God's grace is a gift. There are no special requirements that we have to fulfil in order to be loved by God. Our heavenly Father has acted through Jesus Christ – though somewhat differently than what is traditionally believed. We are not saved through his death, but rather, as shown in the book, through following his life-giving teachings about the availability of God's Love. We become saved by praying to the Father for the reception of the Divine Love and letting it progressively transform our souls.

By accepting and *responding to God's call* in faith, we will be forgiven and raised above the law of compensation, cause and effect, or judgment. This means that at a certain point in our progression, the consequences for our sins and shortcomings will no longer come to haunt us after our death, when we enter the spirit world. Our response includes following the God-given path to salvation, and by doing that, we will transcend and be freed from the ultimate penalties of the law of compensation.

The more we develop into God's likeness at the soul level, the more we'll "walk in the Spirit" – be motivated by the Divine Love in our daily actions – and reap blessings as a result. Being justified and growing in the Divine Love and nature will not, however, make us immune to suffering and the challenges of earthly life. In fact, trials are stepping stones and provide opportunities for growth during this period of spiritual gestation.

Introduction

Glorification – Finally, we will reach a state when we are "*glorified*". This is when our souls are fully transformed by the Divine Love from the image of God – the state in which they were created – into the divine substance of God. This soul transformation is referred to as the New Birth. It prepares us for entrance and habitation in the Celestial Kingdom of God, where, as divine angels, we will have glorious bodies and countenances. We'll each be given a dwelling of unimagined beauty and have unlimited opportunities for happiness, growth and service. Theoretically, it is possible to achieve this state in this life, but few do.

Part I – The Calling

The calling includes concepts and processes like soul awakening, soul enlivening, or soul opening, as well as a radical change of heart. It is also a drawing and enabling that may need to come from beyond. Naturally and without such awakening, humans are generally not interested in the things of God. By excessively pursuing material knowledge, many neglect their souls, which can get into such a state of inertia or lethargy, that, as far as being a part of the person's activities, the soul may as well be dead. (TGRABJ/2/56)

If a soul is starved and in such condition of stagnation that all its receptive powers are for all practical purposes dead, only some great miracle or unusual ministration can awaken it. But as soon as the light breaks into that soul or mind, and the person/spirit begins to see a way to reach higher levels and expand, he or she will desire to progress. With that desire will also come help in abundance. The person's will then becomes a great force in their progress, and work in conjunction with the help that calls it into operation. (TGRABJ/1/122 and 2/50).

Salvation – redemption from the penalty of the law of compensation, becoming immortal, and being given a home in the Celestial Kingdom of God – is all due to soul transformation by God's Divine Love. To receive the freely available gift of God's Love, however, humans must, through soulful communication to their heavenly Father, show a sincere and earnest desire for it. When God hears their call, He opens up their soul to His Holy Spirit which delivers the Divine Love into their souls. With continued desire and prayer for God's Love, as well as help and influence of spirit guides and teachers, the person will keep progressing in their soul transformation from divine image into divine substance.

Through His mercy and love, God has offered humanity a part of Himself – His Divine Love and immortality. This offer is available to every human soul – both in this life and beyond. Once they realize that this is so, it is up to each individual to decide whether or not to accept the Divine Love and seek it in the required way. To accept, the person needs to pray with all the earnestness and sincere longing of his/her soul to receive God's Divine Love. Chapter 1 elaborates on this further.

Chapter 1: Soul Awakening, New Heart, and Repentance

This chapter shows how a sin-filled soul is a dead soul which needs to come to an awakening (an aspect of the New Birth) in order to be receptive to the path of salvation. It points out how the Old Testament prophecies of the new heart became fulfilled in Jesus' coming to announce and exemplify the availability of the Divine Love. Two kinds of repentance – that exhorted to by John the Baptist and that called to by Jesus – are contrasted, as are the old and new covenant.

State of an Unawakened Soul

A soul in a state of sin and error is not responsive to the inflowing of the Divine Love imparted by the Holy Spirit. Therefore, to get into a state of receptivity, it must be *awakened to its condition of enslavement by sin.* Until such awakening occurs, receiving the Love of God is impossible. Neither is such soul open to turning its thoughts to God's truths and practices of life that will help it progress towards a condition of freedom.

The awakening doesn't come through the Holy Spirit, but must come from other causes that influence the mind, as well as the soul. The person has to arrive at the realization that their life is not in accord with the laws of God, or with the real longings of their heart and soul. Until such awakening takes place, the soul is dead as far as consciousness of the truths regarding its redemption is concerned. Such death means a continuance in thoughts and desires of sin and evil, and in a life which beyond death will lead to long years of suffering. When the awakening occurs, the Holy Spirit can fulfil its mission and bestow the Father's Love into that soul. (Based on TGRABJ/1/113)

Pre-Requisite to Receiving Divine Love

Paraphrased, TGRABJ/1/317 tells us: *No one can come to the Father's Love, except they be born again.* This is the fundamental truth which humans must learn and believe, for *without this New Birth one cannot partake of the divine essence of God's Love,* which makes a person at one with the Father. This Love comes to an individual through the Holy Spirit, which causes it to flow into and progressively fill the heart and soul, so that ultimately all sin and error, which tends to make the person unhappy, is eradicated.

Here the New Birth is equated with the soul awakening and condition for the Holy Spirit being able bring the Divine Love into the heart and soul of a person. Elsewhere, we learn that the New Birth is the end-result of the transformation, when the soul has become fully changed from divine image into divine substance. So we can conclude that as in the Greek, the word *genao* denotes the entire process from conception to birth, the spiritual New Birth can be regarded in the same way. It spans from the first soul opening (of which many may be initially unaware), to a full soul transformation and complete atonement with the Father.

The gospel of John echoes the truth regarding the ability to receive Jesus' teaching and be open to the Divine Love:

John 6:44-45, 65 – "No one can come to me [Jesus] unless the *Father who sent me draws him,* ... It is written in the Prophets: 'They will all be taught by God.' Everyone who listens to the Father and learns from him comes to me [and receives my teaching.] ... [Jesus] went on to say, "This is why I told you that no one can come to me unless the *Father has enabled him.*"

With the initial opening of the soul, followed by soul transformation by the Divine Love imparted by the Holy Spirit comes *receptivity to spiritual knowledge and development of soul perceptions* – understanding at the soul level of what cannot be grasped by the mind.

A Path to Awakening

Some people's soul condition may not be conducive for them to actively pursue the path of salvation through the Divine Love, but they may be more naturally attracted to a path of morality taught by spiritual teachers like the Buddha, Confucius and others. Even the teachings of Jesus were twofold. While bringing the truth of salvation through the Divine Love, for those unable to understand his higher spiritual truths, he gave principles, which if followed, would make them better men and women and help them develop their natural love. Such teachings, even today in churches and elsewhere, may turn the hearts and minds of hearers to spiritual things. This in turn may open their souls to the influence of Celestial spirits, and from this may follow the longings for the Love of the Father.

Everything that helps people progress towards a way of love is commendable. The Divine Love operates at the soul level, and frequently comes into a person's soul without their intellectual understanding of what it is. All humans are children of God by creation, and if they will not become His beloved children in the divine sense (by possessing His substance and nature), He wants them to become the pure and perfect beings that the first parents were before the fall. (Based on TGRABJ/3/303)

New Heart and New Covenant

The Bible sheds further light on the truth of heart transformation. Old Testament prophets Jeremiah and Ezekiel foresaw people receiving *a new heart* – which Jesus later equated with receiving the Divine Love. As the scriptures below and other passages show, the new heart would lead to a radical change in the relationship between God and the individual, abolish the old covenant based largely on letter-of-the-law obedience, and establish the new covenant wherein *the law written in the heart* through the Divine Love would motivate to loving actions. This heart change would enable doing what is right from within in contrast to striving to keep the law and do the right thing based on just will power and through one's own strength.

Old Testament history proves that the Israelites, with, and despite, all their good intentions to obey God, failed time after time when relying on their own will power and strength to obey God's commandments. The result was repeated cycles of promises to obey, rebellions against God, consequences of disobedience in the form of oppression by enemies and other curses, repentance and crying out to God for help, and deliverance out of trouble. Not only does disobedience to, and lack of harmony with, God's laws bring suffering here and now, but after death, in the spirit world, everyone is destined to reap the penalties of the law of compensation. More on this point, and how the law of compensation can be transcended, later.

Ezekiel 36:26-27 – "I will give you a *new heart* and put a *new spirit* in you; I will remove from you your heart of stone and give you a heart of flesh. And I will put my Spirit [my Love] in you and *move you to follow my decrees and be careful to keep my laws.*" [This can be interpreted to mean that when a person accepts God's Love (i.e., receives the new heart), they will naturally come into harmony with God's laws rather than being motivated by fear and relying on their own will and strength to obey.]

Jeremiah 31:31 ... "I will make a *new covenant* with the house of Israel and with the house of Judah. It will not be like the covenant I made with their forefathers when I took them by the hand to lead them out of Egypt, because they broke my covenant, though I was a husband to them," declares the LORD. "This is the covenant I will make with the house of Israel after that time," declares the LORD. "I will *put my law in their minds and write it on their hearts.* I will be their God, and they will be my people. No longer *will a man teach his neighbor, or a man his brother, saying, 'Know the LORD,' because they will all know me."*

A similar language is used in the New Testament book of Romans:

Romans 2:13-15 – For it is not those who hear the law who are righteous in God's sight, but it is those who obey the law who will be declared righteous. (Indeed, when Gentiles, who do not have the law [they didn't receive all the laws and instructions that Israel did], do by nature things required by the law, they are a law for themselves, even though they do not have the law, since they show that the *requirements of the law are written on their hearts*, their consciences also bearing witness, and their thoughts now accusing, now even defending them.)

The gift of a new heart (God's Love), if accepted, has the ability to profoundly change a person's relationship with God. The individual is no longer reliant upon their own self to overcome sin and follow God's laws. By partaking of the new heart, they partake of God's divinity which changes their soul from being created in the image of God into the very essence of Him. This transformation results in naturally living in harmony with God's laws.

To reiterate, the new covenant is of the spirit or inner transformation, and is based on love. By contrast, the old covenant was of the letter or written code and based on law keeping. We are also told that the letter kills while the spirit gives life (Romans 2:29; 2 Corinthians 3:6). The law only pointed to, or was a shadow of, ultimate spiritual realities (Hebrews 10:1). With the advent of the new covenant, the old covenant becomes obsolete (Hebrews 8:13).

Even though we are in the new covenant dispensation, some Christians still have the mentality of the Jews and Pharisees in Jesus' time. They tend to judge others based on how well they keep laws – be it biblical laws and/or church laws and traditions. Judgement and criticism is often unloving and leads to divisiveness, discrimination and disunity. We are exhorted not to judge (Luke 6:37, Matthew 7:1-5), and reminded that as followers of Jesus in God's Love, we are all one body (Ephesians 4:1-6).

Repentance

Repentance involves coming to recognize one's sinful behaviors and wanting to change and to follow God's way. It is turning around, or returning to God – which is what the Old Testament prophets so often exhorted the people of Israel and Judah to do. This was also the repentance preached by John the Baptist in preparing the people for Jesus' message. We read in the gospel of Mark:

Mark 1:2-8 – It is written in Isaiah the prophet: "I will send my messenger ahead of you, who will prepare your way – a voice of one calling in the desert, 'Prepare the way for the Lord, make straight paths for him.'" And so John came, baptizing in the desert region and *preaching a baptism of repentance for the forgiveness of sins*. The whole Judean countryside and all the people of Jerusalem went out to him. Confessing their sins, they were baptized by him in the Jordan River. ... This was [John's] message: "After me will come one more powerful than I, the thongs of whose sandals I am not worthy to stoop down and untie. I baptize you with water, but he will baptize you with the Holy Spirit."

We read further in Mark's gospel:

Mark 1:14-15 – After John was put in prison, Jesus went into Galilee, proclaiming the good news of God. "The time has come," he said. "The kingdom of God is near. *Repent and believe the good news* [of the re-bestowal of the Divine Love that will open to its recipients God's Kingdom]!"

In another source (NTR-4), we learn of the difference between the repentance preached by John the Baptist and by his younger cousin, Jesus.

John preached repentance in the traditional sense of the word – turning away from sin and error and renewed obedience to the Law of Moses, with love of God and one's neighbor. This leads to the condition of the perfect natural man. Jesus also preached repentance, but he meant *a turning anew to God and seeking the Celestial Kingdom of God through prayer*. He taught that God had re-bestowed upon humankind the great gift of immortality in his person, and that *the soul's yearning for God's Love and seeking this Love through earnest prayer was real repentance.* When he said, "I have not come to call the righteous but sinners to repentance," (Luke 5:32), he meant that by turning to God, sinners, as well as the righteous, could receive the gift of the Divine Love. But while it was available to both, it was not the righteous in Jesus' day, but the sinners who repented and sought God and His Love. Unfortunately, the righteous, or those who considered themselves righteous, refused in their self-satisfaction the great gift that was theirs for the asking.

In the Acts of the Apostles following Jesus' death, we read about Peter telling a crowd of onlookers that gathered after witnessing the miraculous healing of a crippled man: "Repent, then, and turn to God, so that your sins may be wiped out." (Acts 3:19).

While a soul is not instantly cleansed by receiving a portion of the Divine Love, *the inflowing of the Love into a person's soul starts them on the way of right thinking and makes them realize that their soul is open to the influence of the Love.* Both mortals and spirits may receive this awakening of divine grace as soon as they recognize that they have sinned and fall under judgment (penalties of the law of compensation), and that this Love is the only thing that will free them from having to pay these penalties. (TGRABJ/2/56). This is the act of repentance, exhorted to by Jesus and his apostles.

Many Christian writers, including John Wesley, also use the term *conversion*. This is a turning around, leaving one orientation for another. It may be sudden and dramatic, or gradual and cumulative. But in any case, it is a new beginning and can also be seen as rebirth, new life in Christ, or regeneration.

The calling / drawing / enabling / awakening / rebirth / regeneration / coming to repentance / being converted / becoming open to receiving the Divine Love / starting on a new life in Christ can all be compared to human conception. The first inflowing of God's Love changes a *child of God by creation* – which we all are because our souls were created by God – into a *true redeemed child of God*. Like the male sperm impregnating the female ovum, the initial amount of the Divine Love has started the person off on a journey to the Celestial Kingdom and immortality by giving them a *new heart, new understanding, new perspective, and new relationship with God.*

In Part II and associated chapters, we'll learn more about forgiveness of sins and justification, both as an event and a process. In fact, while the "events" discussed in this chapter can be compared to spiritual conception, Part II will discuss "spiritual gestation" – a process that can continue throughout this life and into the next, and varies in length for different individuals.

Part II – Justification

As mentioned, all humans after this life pass on into the spirit world and become subject to the *law of compensation*. It is the law of cause and effect – all wrong actions and law-breaking bring about penalties that will have to be paid. Jesus and others in the Bible referred to this process on numerous occasions as *judgment*.

Matthew 12:36 – But I tell you that men will have to give account on the day of judgment for every careless word they have spoken.

In TGRABJ/2/56 (paraphrased), we find the same in different words. No one can save themselves by their own efforts from the operation of the law of compensation. This law of cause and effect operates automatically and relentlessly. Every time we sin – break any of the laws of conduct summed up by loving God and loving neighbor – there is a penalty. This penalty may not come immediately or even in this life, but ultimately will have to be paid.

As these penalties are paid, soul purification occurs and the person progresses nearer and nearer to a time and condition when the law of compensation will cease to operate on them. The purer their soul becomes, the more happiness they will experience. However, such payment and resultant soul purification may require long years of suffering. For every wrong deed, and for not doing what should have been done, each person will have to answer the law.

Other Bible passages refer to our human predicament that brings judgment or penalties of the law of compensation as curse or imprisonment:

Galatians 3:10, 22; 4:3 – All who rely on observing the law are under a curse, for it is written: 'Cursed is everyone who does not continue to do everything written in the Book of the Law' [because as soon as the law is broken, penalty ensues]. ... The Scripture declares that the whole world is a *prisoner of sin* [of which we can free ourselves only through a long period of expiation.]

Yet, there is a hope. Again, in TGRABJ/2/56, we are told that while the penalties of the law of compensation cannot be avoided under ordinary circumstances, there is one exception: This is *"the redemption of a man's soul by the Love of the Father entering into it, and making it at-one with His own, and like His in all the qualities that partake of the divine essence."*

The chapters in Part II deal with the various aspects of this redemption / justification through the Father's Divine Love, how it works in this life, and what part each person has to play.

Divine Love Journey as Gestation

Those on the Divine Love journey are in the process of development which can be compared to gestation – the

Part II – Justification

prenatal development in the womb. Physically, the unborn embryo / fetus is already a child of its parents. In about nine months, it will be ready to be born into a very different environment, but its growth and development will continue.

On the spiritual level, we are at this stage true children of God and going, with our cooperation and effort, through a process involving justification, purification and transformation, and indeed re-creation, until our soul development reaches such level that we will be born into the Celestial Kingdom of God.

We learn in TGRABJ/2/56 (paraphrased) that there is no immediate transformation upon the Divine Love entering the soul of a sinner. The person doesn't straight away become a saint or all at once get rid of their evil nature, for such an instantaneous cleansing would not serve the purpose for which the work of the redemptive Love is intended. Some, however, seem to be able to receive more of this Love in a short time than others, and so their redemption is more quickly accomplished.

While most churches teach that the blood of Jesus cleanses from all sin, and that it happens in the twinkling of an eye, this is not true. Jesus' blood was spilled centuries ago, and having become a part of other elements of the natural world, it cannot save anyone. Jesus himself never taught that his blood could save or that the shedding of his blood was in any sense the means of saving a soul. Sadly, this prevalent, but untrue teaching takes people's attention away from the one vital principle that is necessary for their salvation. This is the New Birth, which means the flowing into a person's soul and becoming a part of it, the Divine Love of the Father. This does not happen because of Jesus' bloody sacrifice, said to appease the wrath and meet the requirements of the Father, or because of any vicarious suffering of Jesus. Rather, it is the Father's gift to whomever asks for it.

Progressive Sinlessness

Every soul on the Divine Love path becomes sinless to the degree that it has received the Father's Love. This substance of God merges with our soul, progressively transforming it into a sinless state (*"incorruptible"*, as 1 Peter 1:23 is sometimes translated; also "imperishable" – NIV – as we shall see later). This process will continue until the soul is so replete with the Divine Love that it experiences a complete transformation. From then on, we will be fully born children of God, and upon passing into the spirit world, glorified inhabitants of the Celestial Kingdom. We will resemble Jesus in his glorified state – though with lesser brightness, for he is the most advanced spirit in the Divine Love and will always have pre-eminence. As we read in John 1:13, we will become *"children born not of natural descent ..., but born of God."*

The next ten chapters deal with this redemption process and its stages of development, which are not necessarily linear. This spiritual gestation includes justification; becoming true children of God; receiving immortality;

being transformed into a new and loving being; experiencing a change of desires; growing in spiritual virtues and understanding; increasing in faith; and being born of water and the Spirit.

Chapter 2 – Two Means to Justification

There are two pathways that lead to an eventual life of happiness. In both cases, humans need to get in harmony with God's laws and purify their souls to reach a state of justification. One is achieved via a long arduous journey through largely human effort. The other is an easier way via accepting God's gift of Divine Love offered purely by grace, being forgiven, and receiving help in having one's soul transformed. Human effort and cooperation are still required, but the path is considerably easier – a light yoke that Jesus offers contrasted with a heavy burden.

This chapter compares the two pathways and explores in more detail the latter way to forgiveness and redemption from the penalties of sin that the law of compensation demands.

Two Ways with Two Different Outcomes

We learn in TGRABJ/1/22 (paraphrased) that the observance of moral precepts and the cleansing of the soul from sin by following these precepts, will not lead to the Celestial Kingdom. Rather this law of obedience and exercising of the natural love will result in restoration of the state in which man was originally created – perfect, but without anything of the divine. This condition of perfection, in harmony with God's will and laws, will lead to a great happiness. Yet, the humans or spirits who reach this state will continue to be only created beings, having nothing more than the image of their Maker.

The difference between the Kingdom of the Perfect Man and the Celestial Heavens illustrates the difference between the missions of the great teachers and reformers who preceded Jesus and the mission that Jesus came to perform on earth. The former could not have taught the way to the Celestial Kingdom, for until Jesus' coming, the Divine Love was unavailable after the first parents lost it, and there was no Celestial Kingdom in existence. Morality by itself cannot give to humans what is essential for transforming their soul from divine image into divine substance (Divine Love). Yet, soul transformation is the necessary condition to enter the Father's Kingdom. Jesus was the first to have undergone this transformation and to enter the Kingdom of his Father.

Hindus and others teach that humans have a divine spark within them, which only needs to be realized. This teaching is in error. The first parents, Amon and Aman (or Adam and Eve according to the Bible record), were created perfect in every way, but were not divine beings. They had a pure soul created in the image of the Father, and were given the opportunity to become divine beings by praying to receive God's Love (symbolized by the Tree of Life in Genesis 2:9). They rejected this opportunity and God subsequently withdrew it (Genesis 3:22-24). Note that this opportunity was a gift coming from God, not already instilled within the first couple.

The Scripture also contrasts two states of justification. The first is by keeping the law and overcoming human weaknesses by one's own efforts – the natural love path – which is a long, arduous process involving the law of compensation. The second is justification by grace and faith in Jesus' message of salvation through the Divine Love. This is a much easier way. Jesus invites those who are willing: "Come to me, all you who are weary and burdened, and I will give you rest. Take my yoke upon you and learn from me, for I am gentle and humble in heart, and you will find rest for your souls. For my yoke is easy and my burden is light." (Matthew 11:28-30).

Romans 5:16-19 compares the two ways: "Again, the gift of God is not like the result of the one man's sin: The *judgment followed one sin and brought condemnation*, but the *gift followed many trespasses and brought justification*. For if, by the trespass of the one man [Adam], death [loss of the potentiality of the New Birth and immortality] reigned through that one man, how much more will those who receive God's abundant provision of grace and of the gift of righteousness [through the Divine Love] reign in life through the one man, Jesus Christ [who taught about and exemplified this gift]. Consequently, just as the result of one trespass was condemnation for all men, so also the result of one act of righteousness was *justification that brings life for all men*. For just as through the disobedience of the one man [Adam] the many were *made sinners* [and subject to judgment or law of compensation], so also through the obedience of the one man [Jesus] the many will be *made righteous* [by forgiveness and transformation by the Divine Love].

Galatians 3:13, 23-24 also tells us: "Christ redeemed us from the curse of the law [the penalties that result from imperfect keeping of the law]. ... Before this faith came [in Jesus' teaching of salvation], we were *held prisoners by the law*, locked up until faith should be revealed. So the law was put in charge to lead us to Christ *so that we might be justified by faith* [faith that God has provided a better way through His Divine Love and that it is available for the asking].

Romans 7:14-23 shows the apostle Paul's struggles with his human nature but comes to a wonderful conclusion: "We know that the law is spiritual; but I am unspiritual, sold as a slave to sin. I do not understand what I do. For what I want to do I do not do, but what I hate I do. And if I do what I do not want to do, I agree that the law is good. As it is, it is no longer I myself who do it, but it is sin living in me. I know that nothing good lives in me, that is, in my sinful nature. For I have the desire to do what is good, but I cannot carry it out. ... For in my inner being [heart/soul] I delight in God's law; but I see another law at work in the members of my body, waging war against the law of my [soul] and making me a prisoner of the law of sin at work within my members. [struggle between mind and soul or between our carnal nature and spiritual nature.]

Paul further continues:

Romans 7:24-8:1 – What a wretched man I am! Who will rescue me from this body of death? Thanks be to God – through Jesus Christ our Lord! So then, I myself in my mind am a slave to God's law, but in the sinful nature a slave to the law of sin. *Therefore, there is now no condemnation for those who are in Christ Jesus,* because through Christ Jesus [his teaching about the Divine Love] the law of the Spirit of life [Divine Love] set me *free from the law of sin and death.*

2 Corinthians 5:17-19 puts it yet another way. As we are transformed by the Divine Love into new creatures by grace, we are also reconciled to God. It then becomes our responsibility to teach others the message of reconciliation through the Divine Love – the gospel that Jesus brought. "Therefore, if anyone is in Christ, he is a *new creation*; the old has gone, the new has come! All this is from *God, who reconciled us to himself through Christ* [Divine Love] and gave us the *ministry of reconciliation*: that God was reconciling the world to himself in Christ, *not counting men's sins against them.* And he has committed to us the message of reconciliation.

In conclusion, Paul crescendos: "What, then, shall we say in response to this? *If God is for us, who can be against us?* .... Who will bring any charge against those whom God has chosen? It is God who justifies [redeems from law of compensation]. ... *Who shall separate us from the love of Christ?* Shall trouble or hardship or persecution or famine or nakedness or danger or sword? ... No, in all these things we are more than conquerors through him who loved us. For I am convinced that *neither death nor life, neither angels nor demons, neither the present nor the future, nor any powers, neither height nor depth, nor anything else in all creation, will be able to separate us from the love of God that is in Christ Jesus our Lord.* [Divine Love that he announced and lived by and taught how to receive and live by, that guarantees us a place in God's Kingdom.] (Romans 8:31-39)

Justification through Divine Love Available for the Asking

The Divine Love is an unearned gift of God – a gift of grace – yet available for the asking. After the first parents rebelled against God, this gift (symbolized by the Tree of Life in Genesis 2 and 3) was withdrawn until the coming to the earth of Jesus. All who lived and died during that period came under the penalty of the law of compensation or judgment. Since Jesus' coming, humans can be, by faith in and application of the message of salvation that Jesus brought, freed from the bondage and penalties of sin. Despite their human shortcomings, through the Divine Love transforming their souls, they progressively become justified, redeemed, no longer under condemnation.

The redeeming Divine Love is promised to all who ask. Our heavenly Father is more than willing to give this precious gift to His earthly children as we read in the gospel of Luke:

Luke 11:9-13 – So I say to you: Ask and it will be given to you; seek and you will find; knock and the door will be opened to you. For everyone who asks receives; he who seeks finds; and to him who knocks, the door will be opened. Which of you fathers, if your son asks for a fish, will give him a snake instead? Or if he asks for an egg, will give him a scorpion? If you then, though you are evil, know how to give good gifts to your children, *how much more will your Father in heaven give the Holy Spirit to those who ask him!*

All we need is faith and earnest soul-longing. In TGRABJ/1/24 (paraphrased) we learn that the only way to God's Kingdom and to justification is a sincere heartfelt belief that the Love of the Father is waiting for, and will not be withheld from, anyone who comes to the Father in faith and heartfelt aspiration. If in addition to this belief, people pray with earnest, soulful longings that God will open up their souls, the Holy Spirit will impart the Love, progressively transforming the soul into the very essence of the Father's Love.

The same message further tells us (paraphrased) that those who believe in the Father's promise and pray will never be disappointed, and the way to the Kingdom is guaranteed to be theirs. No mediator is needed, nor are the prayers or ceremonies of priests or preachers, for God Himself hears this kind of prayers and responds by sending the Comforter, the Holy Spirit, which conveys the Divine Love into human souls.

The Bible again echoes the same thought. In the book of Hebrews, we read that "anyone who comes to God must believe that He exists and that he rewards those who earnestly seek him." (Hebrews 11:6). And when our souls diligently seek Him, Romans 5:5 tells us that "hope does not disappoint us, because *God has poured out his love into our hearts by the Holy Spirit*, whom he has given us." According to Mark Kramer, "poured out", in other Bible versions translated "shed abroad", comes from Greek *ekkecutai*, which means that *it has been, and continues to be* poured out or shed abroad. It is an ongoing and continuous process dependent only on our prayers and willingness to receive.

Immediate and Ongoing Justification

Justification through the Divine Love can be seen as both an event and a process. According to John Wesley, true justification happens when Christians abandon their vain attempts to justify themselves before God, to be seen as "just" in God's eyes through religious and moral practices. It is a time when *God's justifying grace* is accepted, a time of pardon and forgiveness, of new peace, joy and love. Indeed, we are justified by God's grace through faith.

With conversion and the Divine Love beginning to work in our hearts and souls, we are no longer under condemnation – though cause and effect still operate in this world. Being justified and growing in the Divine Love will bring us blessings, but it will not make us immune to suffering and the challenges of earthly life. In fact, trials are often blessings in disguise – stepping stones on the way of progression. They can be regarded in a positive way (the Bible, in James 1:2-4, even mentions joy) because they provide opportunities for growth during this period of spiritual gestation.

Justification continues as we are praying for the Divine Love, and as a result, our soul is becoming transformed and increasingly more purified and at-one with the Father. The more we develop into God's likeness through soul transformation, the more we'll "walk in the Spirit" – be motivated by the Divine Love in our daily actions. It is a journey of ongoing repentance — continually turning away from behaviors rooted in sin or worldly pursuits, and toward attitudes and actions that express God's Love.

How Divine Love Brings About Justification

The following paraphrased TGRABJ excerpts show how the Divine Love works in the process of justification, and at what point we become redeemed and above the law of compensation.

In TGRABJ/1/312 we learn that God is a God of love, and no one can come to Him (in the sense of becoming at-one with Him) unless they receive the Love of the Father in their soul. Humans, with their natural inclination to error and violation of God's laws, *can be redeemed from sin and saved only by obtaining this Love* through prayer and faith in God's willingness to bestow it upon the seeker. To be effective, the prayer needs to emanate from the person's soul and not be a mere intellectual desire. The intellect is not the faculty that unites a person with God. Only the soul is made in the likeness of the Father's soul, and unless this likeness is transformed into the substance of God by a filling of the soul with the Divine Love, it remains a mere likeness or image of the Father.

God's Love is the only thing that can unite God and a human. This Love is not a part of man's natural existence, and without it, it is impossible to enter the Celestial Spheres. It is received through the ministrations of the Holy Spirit – the only instrument of God's workings used to bring about human salvation.

When on earth, Jesus taught the way of salvation through the Divine Love. Mere belief in Jesus or in his name will not enable anyone to receive this Love of the Father or be saved. Hence his saying that "all sins against me or against God's commandments may be forgiven men, but the sin against the Holy Spirit will not be forgiven them, neither on earth nor in the spirit world." This means that *as long as one rejects the Spirit's influence, they sin against it, and such sin prevents them from receiving the Divine Love.* While in that state, *they cannot be forgiven, reach the state of justification and redemption,* and be permitted to enter into the Father's Celestial Kingdom. Such person is *subject to the law of compensation (judgment)* and will have to pay all the penalties for his sins that the law imposes.

God's Love does not need the human love to give this love a divine essence. Rather, the human love, to become divine in nature, must be absorbed by the Divine Love. Human love is but a shadow of the Father's Love, and as long as a person refuses to receive the Divine Love, they will remain apart from the Father, and enjoy only the happiness which the natural love affords.

We read further in TGRABJ/2/28 and 2/29 that received in sufficient amount, the Divine Love *eradicates desires for what is not in harmony with God's laws.* This is what repentance is about – turning from sin and desiring the things of God.

Also, a sufficient abundance of the Divine Love will result in *sins being blotted out.* This is *the law of regeneration.* Otherwise, there would be no difference between the person who continues without this Love and the one who receives it, and the New Birth would mean nothing. So, not only is this Great Love sufficient to cleanse the soul of the results of the sins of earth life, but it does this when one is a mortal.

While the law of recompense or compensation certainly exists, there is a higher law that nullifies that law. When the Divine Love enters the soul of a mortal, that which the law of compensation operates upon is removed from the scope of its working, for Love is the fulfilling of the law.

Elaborating on this a little more, it can be said that because the Divine Love is cleansing us from the effects of what we have done wrong and from our soul encrustations, we don't have to recompense someone on earth who we may have harmed. This is the idea behind the Divine Love removing that which can activate the law of compensation. God's Love purifies our soul and removes little by little the energies associated with our unloving thoughts or actions. We may retain the memories of our acts, but not the pain and negative emotions of the party whom we have wronged.

The suffering brought about by the law of compensation is the result of, in a way, reliving from the perspective of the party we have harmed, the non-loving act. The law of compensation shows us in this way how our bad deeds have affected others. This, however, is nullified with receiving God's Love. The memory of the act remains, but the law of compensation isn't activated for us to feel the pain of the other.

TGRABJ/2/34 provides further insight into how the Divine Love frees us from the penalties of the law of compensation. Since upon receiving a sufficient amount of God's Love, all sin that we have committed will be blotted out, there will be no more penalties to pay for our sinful deeds.

When Jesus said, "as you sow, so shall you reap", he meant this law to be applied to the natural man, as well as to everything in nature. But that law is subject to being set aside as far as its operation on souls receiving in sufficient abundance the Divine Love. When this happens, the law of compensation is made non-effective and the law of Love becomes supreme, and man is relieved from the penalties of their sins.

In TGRABJ/2/29, we are further told that it is possible to progress in the Divine Love on earth just as rapidly as in the spirit world. Father does not require the child of His care to be in the spirit world in order to develop their soul. Our soul doesn't change when we pass over, and so we can let God fill it with His Love while on earth. It all depends on each of us individually.

All souls must answer for the sins done in the body, but it is not necessary that the penalties be paid in the spirit world. The reaping of what has been sown can be done while on earth. The more earnestly we seek for and obtain God's grace and Love on earth, the greater will be our progress in the spirit world.

Upon entering the Third Spirit Sphere, there is no longer a need for expiation or purification as occurs in the lower spheres. This sphere is one of great happiness – to keep increasing with further progression – and here one becomes a redeemed spirit. (See also TGRABJ/3/36.)

We'll conclude this section with an account from Perry Ross, who by praying for the Divine Love after death progressed from a dark sphere to, as of the writing (TGRABJ/3/401), close to the Third Spirit Sphere. He also explains how the Divine Love transcends the law of compensation.

"I shall soon be in the Third (Spirit) Sphere, so the spirit friends who have been so kind and loving to me, tell me. It gives me much happiness to know that such a prospect is opened up to me, for I can, because of the progress that I have already made, realize to some extent what a home in that sphere will mean to me." Perry further comments, "I am very happy now, and my sufferings have left and I know that all these blessings came to me because of the workings of the Divine Love in my soul. It is wonderful what that Love can accomplish in the way of rescuing a sinful soul from its surroundings of darkness and from suffering.

"The law of compensation, which is a great truth, does its work without hesitation or partiality, or interference by any God or angel in the way of commanding it to cease its work, but this great Divine Love is more powerful than the law, and when it enters into the soul of a man or spirit, it in effect says to this law: 'You shall no longer operate on the soul of the sinner that was, because I [Divine Love] will take that soul away from and outside the operations of the law.'"

In other words, the Divine Love does not set aside the law, but merely removes that upon which the law operates. So while the law never ceases to operate until the penalties that are called for are paid, this Love is above the law, though not antagonistic to it, and thus transcends it.

Law of Liberty

On more than one occasion, Jesus confronted the Pharisees and the teachers of the law about hypocrisy – outward appearance of righteousness, but inward pride, greed, self-indulgence, and lack of love. They were also corrected for laying heavy burdens on the people that they themselves weren't willing to bear – in the form of legal requirements. Jesus didn't so much correct them for their meticulous law-keeping as for their hypocrisy and for neglecting the more important matters of justice, mercy and faithfulness. Their conduct was a stumbling block to those who sincerely sought God. Ultimately, the Pharisees would be held accountable for causing others to stumble and for hindering their spiritual progress (Matthew 23:2-28; Luke 11:39-46).

By contrast to the heavy legalistic burdens of the Pharisees, Jesus invited the weary to follow a new and easier way: "Come to me, all you who are weary and burdened, and I will give you rest. Take my yoke upon you and learn from me, for I am gentle and humble in heart, and you will find rest for your souls. For my yoke is easy and my burden is light." (Matthew 11:28-30).

Compared to the proud Pharisees, Jesus exemplified a way of humility. He came to serve, not to be served (Matthew 20:28; John 13:13-15). His followers were to obey him and to follow his example. He gave them a new, yet old, command – to love one another. The Old Testament taught love for God and love for neighbor (Leviticus 19:18; Deuteronomy 30:16). But Jesus taught them a new way to love – to love as he loved them, with God's Divine Love. This way, loving one's neighbor was not burdensome, being a natural result of the Divine Love transforming the soul (1 John 2:3-11; 5:2-3).

The truth that the Law of Love frees us from judgment or the law of compensation – reaping the results of our sinful actions from this life in the spirit life is also found in the book of Romans:

Romans 8:1-7 – Therefore, *there is now no condemnation for those who are in Christ Jesus [Divine Love], because through Christ Jesus [Divine Love], the law of the Spirit of life [Divine Love] set me free from the law of sin and death [the specific commandments which define sin, and down the line also the law of compensation]. ... And so he condemned sin in sinful man, in order that the righteous requirements of the law might be fully met in us, who do not live according to the sinful nature but according to the Spirit.* [Through the Divine Love that came with Jesus – not his sacrifice – the law of compensation is superseded. Divine Love in the soul replaces sin and thus fulfils/transcends the requirements of the law.]

Two Means to Justification

The concept of freedom continues in the book of Galatians with a note of caution.

Galatians 5:13-18 – You, my brothers, were called to be free. *But do not use your freedom to indulge the sinful nature; rather, serve one another in love.* The entire law is summed up in a single command: "Love your neighbor as yourself." So I say, *live by the Spirit [Divine Love], and you will not gratify the desires of the sinful nature.* For the sinful nature desires what is contrary to the Spirit, and the Spirit what is contrary to the sinful nature. They are in conflict with each other, so that you do not do what you want. *But if you are led by the Spirit, you are not under law [the law is fulfilled and transcended].* (See also Luke 4:18 and 1 Peter 2:16)

So the highest law is the Law of Love, and the path of Divine Love, whereby our soul is being transformed, is also a law of liberty. It frees us from carrying heavy burdens of meticulous law keeping, from judgment (law of compensation), and therefore from fear of punishment.

1 John 4:18 – *There is no fear in love.* But perfect love drives out fear, because fear has to do with punishment. The one who fears is not made perfect in love.

Truly, perfect love – walking in the Divine Love and being justified by faith in God's grace – drives out the torment of fear and makes us free indeed.

Two Means to Justification

In TGRABJ/1/312, we further learn that spirits who possess the Divine Love become, as it were, a part of divinity and will never be subject to temptation or unhappiness. They will be free from all powers that might lead them to unhappiness, sin, or loss of divinity. The Love makes a mortal and sinful person an immortal and sinless spirit, destined to live through all eternity in the presence of and at one with the Father.

In summary, there are two ways of reaching a state of forgiveness and justification, both requiring human effort. The first is a demanding, self-powered way of overcoming sin and keeping the law in all its facets. The second is an easier, God-assisted way by grace and through faith, and involves soul transformation by the Divine Love, whereby the individual progressively becomes a new creature. The choice as to which way to follow is ours, and the Divine Love is available to all who sincerely seek it and ask.

In following the easier way, justification starts with conversion and the initial inflowing of God's Love. However, it is a process continuing varying lengths of time, depending on each individual. It is completed when the soul is sinless and the law of compensation has nothing more to operate on. This law is then set aside and transcended by the highest law, the Law of Love. It occurs when the soul condition reaches the level of the Third Spirit Sphere, at which point one is a redeemed spirit. It is possible for our souls to reach this state and operate at this level even in the physical life. This may be something to strive for, since the more progress we make on earth, the faster our progress will be in the spirit world.

Chapter 3 - Our Status as True Children of God

The New Birth is the rebirth of the human soul through the Divine Love, and it makes us true children of God. This chapter shows what this entails and how those on the Divine Love path differ from those on the natural love path in their status as God's redeemed children.

From the time that we start receiving the Divine Love, we have a part of God within us. Going back to our stages of birth analogy, in a sense we are a begotten child of God, having a small amount of divine substance in our soul. We then start on a journey of soul transformation into more and more of God's likeness till eventually we become totally at one with our heavenly Father and born into the Celestial Kingdom of God – though as shown later, we will never become God or equal to God.

Our status is now different to those not converted and not on the Divine Love Path. While they too are children of God – beloved and cared for – they do not have anything divine in them. They are God's children by creation – their soul was created by God in His image, and they have been given life by God – but not divine nature. Perhaps an analogy, though imperfect as all analogies are, would be a person creating a doll. It is made in the image of its creator, but doesn't have their substance in the same way that a biological child does. So the doll is not a true child. If it could become human and receive the life and nature of its creator, it would then be a true child.

The Only Way to Become God's True Child

In TGRABJ/1/296, Jesus tells us: "To [John] I explained my real mission and taught him the spiritual truths which I came to teach, and the only way in which mortals could receive that *Love of the Father, which was necessary to make them one with the Father and enable them to partake of the divinity of the Father*. Hence, only in John's Gospel is written *the one necessary requirement to a full salvation and redemption of mankind ... that men must be born again in order to enter into the Kingdom of Heaven*. This is the only true way by which a man can *become a true child of the Father, and fitted to live in and enjoy the Father's Kingdom to the fullest*. The other disciples had more or less conception of this necessary truth, but not the full comprehension of what it involved. Peter was more possessed of this Love than were the other disciples, except John, and with it *he also understood that I was the true son of my Father*."

The Prayer Perfect (TGRABJ/1/40 and following Chapter 12 in this book) also shows this difference in status as God's children:

Our Father, in the Celestial Heaven, we recognize You as all Holy, loving and merciful, and *we as Your children, are not the subservient, sinful or depraved creatures the teachers of old would have us believe. We are the greatest and most wonderful of all Your creations, and the objects of Your great Soul's Love and tenderest care.* [All of humanity are God's beloved children irrespective of race, gender, or religious beliefs. He loves everyone equally. However, before partaking of God's Love, they are only children by creation, not by being begotten/born.]

Your will is that we become at-one with You, and partake of the great Love bestowed upon us through Your mercy and desire that we become, in truth, Your children through Love, not through the sacrifice and death of any of Your creatures. [When we partake of God's Love/substance, we become His true children.]

We pray that You will open up our souls to the inflowing of Your Love, and then will come *the Holy Spirit to bring into our souls Your Divine Love in great abundance, until we are transformed into the very essence of Yourself. Then will come to us such faith as will cause us to realize that we are truly Your children, and one with You in very substance, and not in image only.* [As we are transformed through the Love into the Father's essence, we receive faith (soulful knowledge) that we are truly God's children – not just creatures.]

In a message received by Dr. David Lampron we read: "You are my disciples, and I love you so dearly. I am aware of your struggles when you have struggles, and I am aware of your happiness when you are greatly fulfilled by the blessings of our Father. For He knows all of you so intimately and *loves you as the true children He wants all of His children to be*; and He understands that, in order for this to take place, *they must understand how to become His true children.*" (Reference at the end of the book.)

God's true children are his *redeemed children* – redeemed not by Jesus' death and blood, but rather by the Divine Love imparted through the Holy Spirit. They are also converted and saved. In TGRABJ/4/184, Robert Ingersoll, a nineteenth-century US orator shares: "You will remember that I had declared to you my conversion to Christianity – I mean the true Christianity of Jesus and to the faith in the Divine Love of the Father. ... I search for them [people/spirits he had taught on the earth], and when I find them I tell them of my great mistakes and try to turn their thoughts to *the true way to become redeemed children of God.*"

Again, in TGRABJ/2/56 we read: "The one and vital principle which is necessary to their salvation ... is the *New Birth: which means merely the flowing into a man's soul and becoming a part of it, of the Divine Love of the Father.* It does not come to a man because the blood of Jesus was a sacrifice, to appease the wrath and requirements of the Father, or because of any vicarious suffering of Jesus."

The Divine Love is a gift purely by grace and it saves / redeems us from the penalties of the law of compensation: "*No man can, of himself, save himself from the penalties of the law of compensation.* ... This law of compensation is as fixed as any of God's laws, and cannot be avoided under any condition or circumstances, except one, and that is *the redemption of a man's soul by the Love of the Father entering into it, and making it at-one with His own, and like His in all the qualities that partake of the divine essence.*"

The Bible affirms that upon accepting God's offer of the Divine Love – rather than Jesus' death on the cross as payment for our sins, as it also erroneously asserts – our relationship to God changes. We become "born (or begotten) of God" in the sense of possessing a part of God and His nature. We are then God's children in the intimate sense of the word, being able to call our heavenly Father "*Abba*", which is an Aramaic word that would most closely be translated as "Daddy."

John 1:12-13 – But as many as received him [Jesus and his teachings], to them He gave *the right to become children of God*, to those who believe in His name [and follow his example of walking in God's Love]; *who were born, not of blood, nor of the will of the flesh, nor of the will of man, but of God.*"

1 John 5:1 – *Everyone who believes that Jesus is the Christ* [anointed by God for a special task – to bring the message and example of Divine Love – and follows Jesus' example] *is born of God,* and everyone who loves the father loves his child as well.

1 Peter 1:23 – ... For you have been *born again*, not of perishable seed, but of imperishable, through the living and enduring word of God [the teaching that Jesus brought about the Divine Love].

1 John 3:1-2 – *How great is the love the Father has lavished on us, that we should be called children of God!* And that is what we are! The reason the world does not know us is that it did not know him. Dear friends, *now we are children of God*, and what we will be has not yet been made known. But we know that when he appears, *we shall be like him, for we shall see him as he is* [in the Celestial Kingdom through soul perceptions].

Now we are children of God. How? By faith in the gospel of Jesus Christ, the Messiah, which includes doing what Jesus taught, namely praying for and receiving the Divine Love. This is both a present and future reality.

Romans 8:14-17 – … Those who are led by the Spirit of God [Divine Love] are sons [children] of God. For you did not receive a spirit that makes you a slave again to fear [judgment], but you received the Spirit of sonship. And by him we cry, "Abba, Father." The Spirit [imparting Divine Love and substance into our souls] himself testifies with our spirit that we are God's children. Now if we are children, then we are heirs – heirs of God and co-heirs with Christ, if indeed we share in his sufferings in order that we may also share in his glory [in the Celestial Kingdom].

Galatians 4:3-7 – So also, when we were children [immature in soul development], we were in slavery under the basic principles of the world. But when the time had fully come [to reveal the truth about the re-bestowment of the Divine Love], God sent his Son [Jesus], born of a woman, born under law, *to redeem those under law, that we might receive the full rights of sons [and daughters].* Because you are sons, God sent the Spirit of his Son into our hearts, the Spirit who calls out, "Abba, Father." So you are no longer a slave [to the law and its penalties], but a son; and since you are a son, God has made you also an heir [to the Celestial Kingdom of God].

Birth, Not Adoption

The phrase "adoption as sons" is used in verse 5 above in some Bible versions as a translation of the Greek word *uiothesia*. Based on the understanding of Anastasios Kioulachoglou, this is a composite word consisting of *uios* – son – and *thesis* – placing. *Uiothesia* therefore means "placing as sons". The context starting in Galatians 3 makes this clear. Galatians 3:23-4:4 speaks about children that were under a schoolmaster. Though children entitled to inherit, they were no different than, and had the place of, slaves*:*

Galatians 4:1-3 – What I am saying is that as long as the heir is a child, he is no different from a slave, although he owns the whole estate. He is subject to guardians and trustees until the time set by his father. So also, when we were children [Greek: *nepioi*, small children not able to speak – not the same as *uioi*, the word translated as "sons" in Galatians], we were in slavery a under the basic principles [NKJV: elements] of the world.

Verses 4-5 tell us what happened next: *But when the time had fully come* [time to re-bestow the Divine Love and potential for immortality], *God sent his Son, born of a woman, born under law, to redeem those under law*, that we might receive the full rights of sons [Greek *uiothesia* – placing as sons.]

The word "but" that starts verse 4 contrasts the two situations. Before the appointed time of the Father had come, we had the place of slaves, being enslaved to the elements of the world. We were under the law which served as schoolmasters, guardians and stewards. We were also slaves to our human weaknesses and as a result subject to the law of compensation. Then the time appointed by the Father came. God sent forth His son, Jesus to bring the truth of the Divine Love, a means to redeem those who were under the law, from having the place of slaves to the place of children.

Galatians 3:23-26 tells us the same in different words: *Before this faith came* [Divine Love teaching that needs to be accepted by faith], *we were held prisoners by the law, locked up until faith should be revealed. So the law was put in charge to lead us to Christ that we might be justified by faith. Now that faith has come*, we are no longer under the supervision of the law. *You are all sons of God through faith in Christ Jesus.*

The law books, Genesis to Deuteronomy, with their symbolic stories and ceremonies pointed to Jesus Christ's coming. Moses spoke about a prophet greater than himself.

Jeremiah and Ezekiel were inspired to prophesy a new covenant and a new heart, and with them a change in people's relationship to the law – transcending the letter of the law to the spirit of the law and beyond.

There was a time "before faith came" – before the re-bestowing of the Divine Love. Humans were in a sense slaves to the law because every infraction brought a penalty – the law of compensation was at work, and still is for those following the path of the natural love. When Jesus came – teaching and exemplifying the Divine Love and faith that is the true path to salvation by grace, not by works of the law – those on this path are no longer under the law and no longer have the place of a slave. Instead they now have the place of a true child of God. The law of commandments has been transcended by the higher law of Love.

The fact that in the above passage of Galatians (and elsewhere), the word *uiothesia* does not mean that God is our adoptive Father can also be attested by other Bible passages. In John 1:12-13, quoted earlier in this chapter, the word "children" is the Greek word *tekna,* meaning "that which is born". This word gives prominence to the fact of birth. The children of God of verse 12 were born of God!

Again, in John 3, we find Jesus and Nicodemus, one of the Jewish teachers, speaking about a second birth.

John 3:3-8 – In reply Jesus declared, "I tell you the truth, no one can see the kingdom of God *unless he is born again.*" [the Greek says "born from above" – see also NIV margin] "How can a man be born when he is old?" Nicodemus asked. "Surely he cannot enter a second time into his mother's womb to be born!" Jesus answered, "I tell you the truth, *no one can enter the kingdom of God unless he is born of water and the Spirit*. Flesh gives birth to flesh, but the Spirit gives birth to spirit. You should not be surprised at my saying, 'You must be born again.' The wind blows wherever it pleases. You hear its sound, but you cannot tell where it comes from or where it is going. So it is with everyone *born of the Spirit*."

Jesus makes clear that two births are available – the physical birth that all people who have ever lived on this earth have taken part in, and another one, which is the prerequisite for entering into the kingdom of God. This is the "birth from above", also often translated as "being born again". This is indeed a second birth and therefore to say that we were born again is valid. The Greek equivalent of "born from above" is another expression to say "born of God who is in above". It is this birth that makes us true children of God and gives us the right to call God our Daddy (Abba, Father).

Partaking of God's Essence

Is the Divine Love truly the essence of our Father? In Peter's second letter we read:

2 Peter 1:3-11 – His divine power [Divine Love] has given us *everything we need for life and godliness* through our knowledge of him who called us by his own glory and goodness. Through these he has given us his very great and precious promises, so that through them *you may participate in the divine nature* and escape the corruption in the world caused by evil desires. For this very reason, *make every effort* to add to your faith goodness; and to goodness, knowledge; and to knowledge, self-control; and to self-control, perseverance; and to perseverance, godliness; and to godliness, brotherly kindness; and to brotherly kindness, love. For if you possess these qualities in increasing measure, they will keep you from being ineffective and unproductive in your knowledge of our Lord Jesus Christ. But if anyone does not have them, he is nearsighted and blind, and has forgotten that *he has been cleansed from his past sins* [justified]. Therefore, my brothers, be all the more eager to make your calling and election sure. For if you do these things, *you will never fall, and you will receive a rich welcome into the eternal kingdom of our Lord and Savior Jesus Christ* [the Celestial Kingdom].

We hear Peter say quite literally, that we "may participate in the divine nature" (NIV) or "be partakers of the divine nature" (KJV). We have been cleansed from past sins – the law of compensation has been transcended. But we have a part to play – we are to make every effort to grow in virtues. It is by cooperation with our heavenly Father that we grow and are transformed. And if we do our part, our success and place in the Celestial Kingdom is guaranteed. What a wonderful promise!

We learn further in Romans 8 that once a person has received the Divine Love, it can never be taken away from him:

Romans 8:37-39 – In all these things we are more than conquerors through him who loved us. For I am convinced that *neither death nor life, neither angels nor demons, neither the present nor the future, nor any powers, neither height nor depth, nor anything else in all creation, will be able to separate us from the love of God that is in Christ Jesus our Lord.*

Paul isn't just saying that we are loved by God (which we are). He speaks about the gift of the Divine Love in terms of *personal possession*. He also refers to it as a thing of substance, that merges with our soul in such a way that *nothing in the present or future will be able to separate us from the Divine Love.* And to underscore that the Divine Love is not a mere divine sentiment of feeling Love towards His children, but rather the real essence of the Father, Paul gives the Love of God locality: *"that is in Christ Jesus"*.

The Divine Love was unavailable between when the first humans rejected God's gracious offer of this gift and Jesus' coming to earth. At a future time, it will again be withdrawn and the opportunity for salvation and immortality in the Celestial Kingdom will end. Those who had not availed themselves of that opportunity will suffer so called "second death", which means they will remain in the spirit world spheres and have no guarantee of immortal life.

In NTR/26, (paraphrased), we find other insights and collaborating information: Even though the privilege of obtaining the Divine Love is to be in the future withdrawn, this will not apply to those in the Celestial Spheres and those who have some of the Divine Love in their souls and are progressing towards the Celestial Heavens. The Father cannot withdraw from a soul His Love and nature once He has bestowed it, for once it is lodged in a soul, it can never be removed. That soul can seek more and more of the Father's nature for all eternity. The Divine Love creates a special kinship with the Father as a result of the at-onement that forms between that soul and the Great Soul of God. This kinship grows ever closer through eternity as more and more of the divine nature is conveyed into the soul.

We also learn in TGRABJ/1/348 (paraphrased): When this Love enters the soul and works the transformation, it never leaves nor disassociates itself from the soul. Its character of divine essence never changes to that of the mere natural love, and where it is present, sin and error have no existence, because it is impossible for this essence to occupy the same parts of the soul at the same time as sin and error.

Divinity never gives way to that which is not divine. Man is working towards the attainment of the divine when he pursues the way provided for obtaining the divine nature. As he advances and obtains a portion of this Divine Love, no matter how small, he can never lose it.

This, however, does not mean that one may not lose the consciousness of this essence in their soul. This occurs frequently as a result of the indulgence of one's carnal appetites and evil desires. And while this Love can never be eradicated by evil acts or wrong beliefs, the soul progress may become stagnant. It may appear as if the Love was non-existent, and sin and error may dominate the person's life.

However, no matter how deep one's depravation may become, a soul that has once received this divine essence cannot be lost. Its dormant condition may, however, delay its manifestation of life and immortality for a long time, and much suffering and darkness may have to be endured by the soul in such condition.

Becoming at One with God

As mentioned, in partaking of the Divine Love and nature, we are becoming at one with God. In his first letter, John puts it this way:

1 John 4:13 – We know that *we live in him and he in us*, because *he has given us of his Spirit*.

In Paul's first letter to the church in Corinth we read:

1 Corinthians 6:17 – But he who unites himself with the Lord is *one with him in spirit*.

Before his death, Jesus told his disciples, as recorded in the gospel of John:

John 17:22-23 – I have given them *the glory that you gave me*, that they may *be one as we are one*: I in them and you in me. May they be brought to complete unity to let the world know that you sent me and I have loved them even as you have loved me [mutual love and unity through the Divine Love].

The Divine Love will make us at-one with God and we become true children of God in a close bond with the Father. This is reiterated in Romans 8:16: "The Spirit Himself bears witness with our spirit that we are children of God." Also, Galatians 4:6: "God sent the Spirit of his Son into our hearts, the Spirit who calls out, "Abba, Father." Our spirit / heart / soul, through its possession of the essence of the Father, bears joint witness with the Spirit that we have become part of God and God's children as a result of having taken on a portion of His divinity. Such is the way of our loving Father, that He seeks no atonement, but at-onement.

As we seek more of God's Love through prayer, as we grow in the virtues listed in 2 Peter 1 and the fruit of the Spirit listed in Galatians 5, we are becoming more and more transformed into God's likeness as we read in 2 Corinthians 3:18: "And we, who with unveiled faces all reflect [or, contemplate] the Lord's glory, are being *transformed into his likeness with ever-increasing glory*, which comes from the Lord, who is the Spirit."

Backtracking to Jesus' words in John 17:22-23, the God-given glory was not a constituent part of Jesus' soul make-up at creation or birth, but had to be acquired in the same manner as prescribed for all humans: by soulful longings for the inflowing of the Divine Love. In Revelation 3:21, we read: "To him who overcomes, I will give the right to sit with me on my throne, just as I overcame and sat down with my Father on his throne." By saying "just as I overcame," Jesus expresses two vital truths: firstly, he had to overcome himself; and secondly, we too can overcome as he overcame, and dwell with him in the Celestial Heavens.

Jesus has received the Divine Love to the highest degree. As a result, of all human souls, he is closest to God, and has been appointed Master over the Celestial Heavens. We are following in the footsteps of our savior and older brother, who will always have pre-eminence in the Love (Colossians 1:18). He is quoted in John 14:6 as saying: "I am the way and the truth and the life. No one comes to the Father except through me." Despite his exalted position, he is a most humble Celestial spirit, and more than happy to assist his brothers and sisters to inhabit the mansions he has prepared for them in the Celestial Kingdom (John 14:2-3).

To sum up, by being partakers of the Divine Love, we are "born of God", partake of God's substance, become at-one with God, and are God's true and redeemed children here and now in a similar way that an unborn child in its mother's womb is the child of its parents. We are being transformed into God's likeness as we grow in grace and virtues, and will reach our full birth when our souls are fully changed into divine substance. This will qualify us to receive a place in the Celestial Kingdom of God.

Chapter 4 – Possessors of Life and Immortality

When Adam and Eve, or the first parents, sinned, they "died". This means they became separated from God and lost the opportunity to receive the Divine Love, which would have given them immortality. As a result of their disobedience, the potential for immortality through the Divine Love was withdrawn from humanity and all were counted "dead in sins" till the time determined by the Father.

That time came with the birth of Jesus, who had a special relationship with God and started receiving the Divine Love from birth. In maturing, he realized that he was called to be the prophesied Messiah (anointed for a special purpose). That purpose was to proclaim the good news about the re-bestowal of the Divine Love resulting in the New Birth. It was in Jesus, that the Old Testament prophecies of the new heart and new covenant were first being fulfilled.

Metaphorically speaking, in the book of Genesis (3:22-24) Adam and Eve, because of disobedience and rejecting God's instruction, were banished from access to the Tree of Life, which would have given them immortality. According to the book of Revelation (2:7 and 22:2, 14), access to the symbolic Tree of Life is restored.

This chapter shows the difference between continued life in the spirit world and immortality, and how those on the Divine Love path are even in their present life possessors of eternal life and immortality.

True Immortality

In TGRABJ/1/53 (paraphrased) we learn that Jesus was more than a mere reformer. He was not only a good and just teacher, but *he was the first true son of God, and His messenger in bringing to the world the truths of immortality through the Divine Love of the Father, and the way to obtain it.* He was indeed the Way and the Truth and the Life as no other teacher before him ever was.

Immortality means much more than a continuation of life. It means *a life that has in it the Divine Love or essence of the Father*. This makes the *spirit divine, and not subject to death of any kind*. No spirit has immortality just because it is continuing to live in the spirit world. Continuity of life in the spirit realms does not equate with immortality. Only at-onement with God provides the divine attribute of immortality.

Humans whose souls have received the Divine Love are immortal and can never cease to exist. They experience the great comfort and blessing of knowing this because they possess an immortal quality of God that can never have an ending. (TGRABJ/1/50).

Before the coming of Jesus, immortality was not available to humankind – even though some believed in it. That belief was based just on hope derived from spirit communication which showed that death had not annihilated the individual. Jesus brought not just hope, but knowledge of the truth. However, the mere fact of Jesus' resurrection does not prove immortality. Only the Father is immortal, and only those to whom He gives His attributes of immortality can become immortal as He is.

The Divine Love – not merely the natural human love – is the key principle of immortality. The possessor of the Divine Love takes on the nature and likeness of the Father and thus a part of divinity. Consequently, they become immortal, and can never be deprived of their divinity.

State of Those without the Divine Love

In TGRABJ/1/47 (paraphrased), we learn about the difference between the human soul that continues its life in the spirit world and the soul that has experienced the New Birth. The latter not only continues living, but its condition makes its extinction an impossibility – even by God, who in the beginning of human existence created that soul.

Human souls did not always exist – they are not eternal, self-existing or independent. Rather, they depend on the will of God for their existence. It could therefore be inferred that in the future, a soul may have served the purpose of its creation and be disseminated into the elements of which it was created.

Myriads of souls in the spirit world are in a condition of perfection which was the state of the first humans at the time of creation, and which God pronounced "very good." But as mortals have no assurance that at some time, the life of their souls will not end, so the spirits who have reached the perfection of their originally created state have no such assurance. While they have hope and belief that continued existence is their destiny, and are in a state of happiness, they do not have the knowledge that they are immortal. Rather they realize that they depend on the will of God for their existence.

God's relationship with these souls is merely that of the Creator and created. By contrast, His relationship with the souls that have received the New Birth and hence the divine nature, is not only as a Creator and created, but also that of a co-equal so far as the quality of immortality is concerned. These souls become self-existing and not dependent on God for their existence. They are His true children by birth, not just by creation. (TGRABJ/1/122).

Immortal Life in the Celestial Kingdom – and Now

The focus of Jesus' teaching was the Kingdom of God or Kingdom of Heaven, as shown by many references in the Gospels. Specifically, he brought the happy tidings (gospel) that every soul praying for, and receiving, the Divine Love could have eternal life in the Celestial Kingdom of God. In a way, this state can be a part of our consciousness and knowledge while still clothed in the flesh.

TGRABJ/1/47 teaches us that true immortality is the condition of the soul which knows that because of its essence and qualities, it can never cease to live.

Several Bible passages show that the eternal life and immortality given to us is not only for the future, but is a present state. For example, the author of Ephesians tells us:

Ephesians 2:6 – And God raised us up with Christ and *seated us with him in the heavenly realms* in Christ Jesus.

Unlike the first parents, Jesus did not turn down the offer of the Divine Love received through fervent prayer, and so became the first human ever to have possessed this substance of the Soul of God. We can read this in 1 John 5.

1 John 5:11-12 – God has given us eternal life, and this life is in his Son. He who has the Son has life; he who does not have the Son of God does not have life.

In Bible language, through the New Birth, as soon as we start receiving God's Love, we "pass from death to life". Indeed, Jesus came so that humans could have – *upon receiving his teachings and applying them* – immortal life. He brought life and immortality to light and became impersonation of the resurrection. This immortal life is both a present and future reality.

Ephesians 2:1-10 – As for you, *you were dead in your transgressions and sins*, in which you used to live when you followed the ways of this world ... gratifying the cravings of our sinful nature and following its desires and thoughts. ... But because of his great love for us, God, who is rich in mercy, *made us alive with Christ* even when we were dead in transgressions — it is by grace you have been saved. And God raised us up with Christ and seated us with him in the heavenly realms in Christ Jesus, in order that in the coming ages he might show the incomparable riches of his grace, expressed in his kindness to us in Christ Jesus. For it is by grace you have been saved, *through faith* [in Jesus' teachings and God's Divine Love saving us] – and this not from yourselves, it is the *gift of God* – not by works, so that no one can boast. For we are *God's workmanship*, created in Christ Jesus to do good works, which God prepared in advance for us to do.

John 10:9-10 – I [Jesus] am the gate; whoever enters through me will be saved. ... *I have come that they may have life,* and have it to the full.

John 11:25-26 – Jesus said to her, "I am the resurrection and the life. He who believes in me [my teachings] will live, even though he dies; and *whoever lives and believes in me will never die* [because they have immortality].

John 5:24-26 – "I tell you the truth, *whoever hears my word and believes him who sent me has eternal life* and will not be condemned [by the law of compensation]; he has *crossed over from death to life* [through the Divine Love entering his soul and planting the seed of immortality]. I tell you the truth, a time is coming and *has now come* [with the re-bestowal of the Divine Love] when the dead [in sins] will hear the voice of the Son of God and those who hear [listen and apply the teachings] will live. For as the Father has life in himself, so He has granted the Son to have *life in himself* [through the Divine Love.]

2 Timothy 1:8-10 – God who has saved us and called us to a holy life – not because of anything we have done but *because of his own purpose and grace*. This grace was given us in Christ Jesus before the beginning of time, but it has now been revealed through the appearing of our Savior, *Christ Jesus, who has destroyed death and has brought life and immortality to light through the gospel.*

1 John 3:14 – We know that we have *passed from death to life*, because we love our brothers [as a result of the Divine Love in our souls]. Anyone who does not love remains in death [doesn't have immortality].

In summary, the potential for immortality was lost to humans when the first parents rebelled against God. Jesus became the Messiah and savior by announcing that the Father has re-bestowed the gift of immortality, and showing the way that individuals can avail themselves of this gift. The only way is by asking for and being transformed by the Divine Love imparted by the Holy Spirit into our souls. The continuation of life in the spirit world is not a guarantee of immortality, only the New Birth provides this state of being. Those without the Divine Love and New Birth will always remain dependent on God's will and sustenance for their continued existence.

Chapter 5 – Anointed by God

Anointing was a common practice in the Old Testament for those who were set aside for a special job or mission. Both priests and kings were anointed for their office. In the book of Isaiah, even the Persian King Cyrus is referred to as God's anointed because he had a special God-given mission and that was to allow the Jewish exiles to return to Palestine and rebuild the Jerusalem temple that the Babylonians had devastated. The word *anointed* means the same as *Messiah*.

We learn in *76 Sermons/Sermon 62* that in the above case, the term "Messiah" was not used in spiritual terms, but referred to Cyrus as a human instrument of God, such as He had used others to punish the people in the past. Cyrus was going to bring about God's will of redemption from exile. Isaiah has God declare: "I will raise up Cyrus in my righteousness: I will make all his ways straight. He will rebuild my city and set my exiles free, but not for a price or reward, says the LORD Almighty." (Isaiah 45: 13).

This chapter shows how Jesus was anointed for his special mission on earth, and how we as his brothers and sisters following in his footsteps are also anointed.

Jesus the Anointed One

The word *Christ* also means an anointed one, the same as *Messiah*. Jesus was anointed for the mission of bringing the message of salvation through the Divine Love.

He revealed through Dr. Daniel Samuels (*53 Revelations/Rev. 51*) that he did not intend to bring a new religion. Rather, he was teaching people that the Father's Love had again become available to humans. This was what the later Greeks and others of the Western world understood by *Christ the anointed of the Father who brought salvation to humanity through his own personality.* It was, however, quickly forgotten or misunderstood, that the word *Christ* stood for the Father's Divine Love, and that the New Birth through the Father's Love unto eternal salvation was at hand. Therefore originally, *Christianity meant the New Birth through the Divine Love.*

Although Jesus' magnificence surpasses that of all spirits, and his love is beyond earthly comprehension, Jesus emphatically declared that the gift of Divine Love was not just for him. Rather, the Father had ordained that every human soul could partake of the divine essence. We read in Jesus' prayer in the Gospel of John:

John 17:26 – "I have made you known to them, and will continue to make you known *in order that the love you have for me may be in them and that I myself may be in them.*"

Paul reiterates the same in Romans 8:29: "For those God foreknew he also predestined to be *conformed to the likeness of his Son, that he might be the firstborn among many brothers.*" Note that Jesus was not the *"only-born"*, or "God's only Son", to be allowed the transformation into the Father's nature (the New Birth), but that he was merely to be the *"firstborn among many brethren"*.

Jesus as the firstborn and the one most filled with the Father's Love has pre-eminence among humans and spirits. In TGRABJ/3/51 and 1/70, we learn that the Father has given Jesus power over all the spirits in the Celestial Kingdom. He is the Master of the Celestial Kingdom (or, in biblical metaphor, the Head of the church or those born anew – Colossians 1:18).

Christ is the spirit of the Father that God gave to Jesus when he anointed him for his earthly mission, or the spirit that manifests the existence of the Divine Love in the soul. In other words, *Christ* is the quality that came to Jesus after he received into his soul the Divine Love and was fully transformed into the essence of the Father. Phrasing it yet differently, *Christ* is the manifestation of God's Love as bestowed upon Jesus and made part of his existence. Jesus then is the *Christ of God* – the anointed spirit and the great dispenser of truths, who brought eternal life and immortality to light. Jesus the spirit is a spirit like other spirits, with his home in the Celestial Heavens.

Christ in You

The term *Christ*, or *Christ in you*, therefore, can be seen as the Divine Love, and specifically the presence of this Love of the Father in one's soul. It is universal and available to all who sincerely seek it through soulful prayer. Jesus became the Christ (anointed) because he was the first to receive the Divine Love into his soul and manifest its existence. He was anointed to teach that this Love, or *Christ principle*, became again available to humankind. Those who avail themselves of it will become at one with the Father in His substance of Love and immortality.

The Bible also tells us, that we have indeed received a special anointing and that "Christ" is living in our hearts through faith. The following verses are quite inspiring:

1 John 2:20-27 – But *you have an anointing* from the Holy One, and all of you know the truth. ... See that what you have heard from the beginning [Divine Love/New Birth teaching] remains in you. If it does, you also will *remain in the Son and in the Father* [by being at one with them through the Divine Love]. And this is what he promised us – even eternal life [immortality].... As for you, *the anointing you received from him* remains in you, and you do not need anyone to teach you. But as *his anointing teaches you about all things* and as that anointing is real, not counterfeit – just as it has taught you, remain in him.

2 Corinthians 1:21-22 – Now it is God who makes both us and you stand firm in Christ. *He anointed us*, set his seal of ownership on us [becoming his true children], and put his Spirit [Divine Love] in our hearts as a deposit, guaranteeing what is to come [inheritance in the Celestial Kingdom].

Ephesians 3:16-3:19 – I pray that out of his glorious riches he may strengthen you with power through his Spirit in your inner being, so that Christ [Divine Love] may dwell in your hearts through faith. And I pray that you, being rooted and established in love, may have power, together with all the saints, to *grasp how wide and long and high and deep is the love of Christ, and to know this love that surpasses knowledge – that you may be filled to the measure of all the fullness of God.* [Wow! Soul perceptions of what the depth of God's Love is and being filled with it.]

Colossians 1:25-27 – … the commission God gave me to present to you the word of God in its fullness – the mystery that has been kept hidden for ages and generations, but is now disclosed to the saints. To them God has chosen to make known among the Gentiles the glorious riches of this mystery, which is *Christ in you, the hope of glory* [the Divine Love truth that will ultimately bring us to the glory of the Celestial Kingdom].

In summary, as Jesus was anointed for the mission of teaching and manifesting the Divine Love, being the firstborn of many to be transformed by the Love, those who follow his teaching and walk in his footsteps also have a special anointing of "Christ in them" and the mission to be examples of Love and light to others.

Chapter 6 – Transformed into a New Being

Salvation is not a static, one-time event. Rather, it is the ongoing experience of transformation at the soul level by God's Divine Love into divine nature. Using the Old Testament reference to the coming bestowal of the Divine Love, we are speaking about a new heart – a "heart transplant" or heart transformation. Theologian John Wesley described this dimension of God's grace as sanctification or holiness.

This chapter compares the natural and transformed states, discusses biblical analogies of the transformation, explores what we can do to aid the transformation, and describes the manifestations of Divine Love in our lives.

Two Mindsets Contrasted

The Bible contrasts where we came from before conversion and where are we going as the Divine Love begins working in our hearts and souls. While we are not to judge and condemn others, we are encouraged to discern. In fact, Scripture advises us to watch the company we keep, as corrupt behaviour in others does rub off, and we are warned to be on guard (1 Corinthians 15:33; Proverbs 22:24-25). We are told in Matthew 7:16-18 that: *"By their fruit you will recognize them. Do people pick grapes from thorn bushes, or figs from thistles? Likewise every good tree bears good fruit, but a bad tree bears bad fruit. A good tree cannot bear bad fruit, and a bad tree cannot bear good fruit.*" Fruit can include our own actions, as well as the results of our ministry to others (2 Corinthians 3:2-6).

A specific listing of "fruit of the Spirit" (spiritual nature, following the highest law) and a contrasting list of "works of the sinful nature" (the natural loveless proclivity) is found in Galatians 5.

Galatians 5:16-26 – So I say, *live by the Spirit*, and you will *not gratify the desires of the sinful nature*. For the sinful nature desires what is contrary to the Spirit, and the Spirit what is contrary to the sinful nature. They are in *conflict with each other*, so that you do not do what you want. But if you are *led by the Spirit* [motivated by Divine Love imparted by the Holy Spirit], you are not under law [the law is transcended]. The acts of the sinful nature are obvious: sexual immorality, impurity and debauchery; idolatry and witchcraft; hatred, discord, jealousy, fits of rage, selfish ambition, dissensions, factions and envy; drunkenness, orgies, and the like. I warn you, as I did before, that those who live like this will not inherit the kingdom of God [the Celestial Kingdom]. But the fruit of the Spirit is love, joy, peace, patience, kindness, goodness, faithfulness, gentleness and self-control. Against such things there is no law. Those who belong to Christ Jesus [have the Divine Love in their souls] have crucified the sinful nature with its passions and desires. Since we live by the Spirit, let us keep in step with the Spirit. Let us not become conceited, provoking and envying each other.

Analogies to and Nature of the Transformation

Jesus used several physical analogies to illustrate the changes in the human soul brought about by the Divine Love. One comparison is what happens to *dough* through the fermenting action of yeast (Luke 13:20-21). Another one is the *mustard seed* that grows from something tiny into something very large (Luke 13:18-19). Jesus also mentions the effect of *new wine* destroying old wineskins (Mark 2:22), and an *unshrunk patch of cloth* destroying an old piece of clothing when washed (Mark 2:21).

In the gospel attributed to John, Jesus talks with a Samaritan woman about partaking of the *living waters* that become "a spring of water welling up to eternal life" (John 4:14). All these sayings convey the idea of something new and powerful entering into a human being in order to change that person from what he or she was into something completely new and different – indeed, *a new creature*.

Like the yeast (or another leavening agent) that is added to dough to initiate change, the Divine Love is deposited into the soul of a person who earnestly longs for it, initiating transformation. It starts changing that soul at a deep level, permeating it little by little as the individual prays for more of God's Love. With our co-operation and God's sanctifying grace, we grow in ability to live as Jesus lived and love as he loved. As we pray, study, worship, and share in fellowship with others of like mind, we deepen our knowledge of and love for God. As we respond with compassion to human needs, we strengthen our capacity to love others. Our inner thoughts and motives, as well as our outer actions and behavior, become more and more aligned with God's will and will testify to our union with God.

How to Grow and Develop

To continue growing, our effort and involvement are required – transformation doesn't occur automatically. As is written in the book of Philippians 2:12-13, "continue to *work out your salvation, ...* for *it is God who works in you* to will and to act according to his good purpose."

After asking for the Divine Love, we are to consciously act according to its promptings. This involves two aspects – being and doing, and includes love for others, oneself and God, as well as gentleness, kindness, patience, generosity, truthfulness, humility, gratitude, service, integrity, acceptance of others, and promoting peace and harmony.

In Ephesians 5:18, we find additional light on this. It reads, "And be not drunk with wine, wherein is excess; *but be filled with the Spirit!*" According to Mark Kramer, in the original Greek, the imperative phrase "be filled" is one word, *pleroo*, which means to *"render full"*, to *"fill up"*. The Greek verb is in the present tense, rather than the aorist – it is an ongoing instruction. We are to be continually filled with the Spirit. However, the verb is also in the passive voice, which means, that being filled with the Spirit is something done to us by God, and to which we submit. Paul is telling us to not be merely possessed of the Spirit as opposed to being drunk with wine, but he is in effect saying, *"See to it that you are continually, and constantly, being filled up with the Spirit!"*

Manifestations of the Divine Love Transformation

Soul transformation through the Divine Love is the only way to qualify for the Celestial Kingdom of God and have a guarantee of immortality. This is the New Birth which "means merely *the flowing into a [person's] soul and becoming a part of it, the Divine Love of the Father.*" It isn't the result of accepting the blood or death of Jesus as a sacrifice for our sins, to appease the wrath and fulfil the requirements of the Father, or because of any vicarious suffering of Jesus – none of which can transform our souls. (TGRABJ/1/308, paraphrased.)

Put in other words, the New Birth is *"brought about by the flowing into [human souls] of this Divine Love, whereby the very nature and substance of the Father [infuses the soul], and wherefrom [humans] cease to be the merely created beings, but become the souls of men [and women] born into the Divine reality of God."* (TGRABJ/2/56.)

It is a *new creation* from above through the operation of the Holy Spirit upon our life – changing our soul through the Divine Love when we truly repent and turn to God.

The New Birth is both a present and future reality. James Padgett was told by Jesus: "Your soul, as you, has been *developed in its spiritual nature* and you have become in closer union with the Father and have partaken to a large extent of His Love, and, to a degree, been transformed into his essence, so that *you have become a very different entity from what you were when your development for our purpose commenced*; ... You are now [progressing] towards the fountainhead of the Father's Love, and *have taken on a part of His immortality,* and it *depends only upon yourself* how rapid your progress shall be towards a complete transformation such as spirits who are inhabitants of the Celestial Spheres, possess. *You need not wait until you come to the spirit world in order to make a rapid progression*, although it will be more difficult for you to progress while in the flesh, as you understand, but *wonderful progress may be made while in the flesh*, and you have been told the secret of this progress." (TGRABJ/1/5.)

The transformation at the soul / heart level is a gradual process and can be almost imperceptible by the individual as it is occurring. Some have experienced a gentle burning in the heart after they have prayed for and received the Divine Love (cf. Luke 24:32). Others may have no conscious physical perceptions. We are all on a unique spiritual path with unique experiences. Everyone is connected to God in his or her own way. Each person is also likely to be guided in ways that are the most beneficial to them and that will motivate them to keep asking for more Divine Love.

If we recognize this Love as a presence and substance that transforms our lives from the inside, this touches every part of our being – our souls, minds and bodies. Though progression is not necessarily linear, over time, the effects of the transformation will become evident on our faces, in how we view others, in how we express ourselves – in everything we do. We'll manifest more and more of the "fruit of the Spirit" listed in Galatians 5:22 as love, joy, peace, patience, kindness, faithfulness, gentleness and self-control.

As we'll discuss in more detail in the next chapter, our perspectives and desires will change, and spiritual pursuits will gain more importance in our lives. Our soul guidance will gain pre-eminence over mental and intellectual reasoning. We'll be receiving more and more spiritual insights through soul perceptions.

The Bible concurs that with the Holy Spirit / God's Love / Christ in us (these terms often denote the Father's gift of saving grace), we indeed become and are becoming a new creature or creation. We are exhorted to "live by the Spirit", which means to follow the promptings of the Divine Love in our hearts and souls as opposed to the physical passions and desires of our mind:

2 Corinthians 5:17 – "Therefore, if anyone is in Christ [has Divine Love], he is a new creation; the old has gone, the new has come!"

We embark on a new way of life – one where ceremonial laws fall by the wayside and rituals, though sometimes helpful, become not necessary. "Neither circumcision nor uncircumcision [and other ceremonies] means anything; what counts is a new creation." "Those who belong to Christ Jesus [walk the Divine Love path] have crucified the sinful nature with its passions and desires. Since we live by the Spirit [Divine Love in our souls motivating us], let us keep in step with the Spirit." (Galatians 6:15; 5:24-25.)

The transformation and development process is further described in the second epistle of Peter.

2 Peter 1:3-9 – His divine power [Divine Love] has *given us everything we need for life and godliness* through our knowledge of him [God] who called us by his own glory and goodness. Through these he has given us his *very great and precious promises* [of Divine Love / immortality / place in the Celestial Kingdom], so that through them *you may participate in the divine nature* and escape the corruption in the world caused by evil desires. For this very reason, *make every effort* [our cooperation is required] to add to your faith goodness; and to goodness, knowledge; and to knowledge, self-control; and to self-control, perseverance; and to perseverance, godliness; and to godliness, brotherly kindness; and to brotherly kindness, love. For if you possess these qualities in increasing measure, they will keep you from being ineffective and unproductive in your knowledge of our Lord Jesus Christ. But if anyone does not have them, he is nearsighted and blind, and has forgotten that he has been cleansed from his past sins [by the law of Divine Love transcending the law of compensation]. Therefore, my brothers, be all the more eager to *make your calling and election sure*. For *if you do these things, you will never fall*, and *you will receive a rich welcome into the eternal kingdom of our Lord and Savior Jesus Christ* [the Celestial Kingdom].

In summary, the New Birth, or transformation of soul by the Divine Love, is a gradual and ongoing, though not always linear, process. Once we begin it, we become a new being and embark on a new way of life with a new orientation. Spiritual soul development, however, is not automatic, but requires our cooperation and effort. While we are transformed and motivated from within by our "new heart", we need to consciously follow its promptings and act in loving ways, even in situations of temptation. We are to grow in love and other virtues, but we have God's help through His Divine Love in our soul to succeed and become more and more at-one with our heavenly Father.

Chapter 7 – Change of Desires and Growth in Virtues

Desires and appetites are the foundation of our actions. Man was created with both animal appetites and spiritual aspirations, and these were originally harmonious with the laws of his creation. However, man's fall and the loss of spiritual aspirations, as well as the perversion of the animal appetites, have resulted in disharmony with these laws, and hence sin. While not created by God, this tendency to sin has become a part of human nature. To become free from this foreign aspect of their being, humans must replace the wrong appetites and desires with those that are in harmony with God's laws. (TGRABJ/2/192.)

This chapter shows how change of desires is another aspect of the transformation by the Divine Love and how this results in growth in virtues.

Transformation of Desires

Led and motivated by the Divine Love within, we'll start desiring the things of God, rather than the things of the world. But conscious choices are still required because following godly desires does not happen automatically and God does not violate our free will. Therefore, on numerous occasions, Bible writers exhort God's children to be aware of their desires and not follow those that are unwholesome.

Romans 6:12 – Therefore do not let sin reign in your mortal body so that you obey its evil desires.

Romans 8:5 – Those who live according to the sinful nature have their minds set on what that nature desires; but those who live in accordance with the Spirit [Divine Love] have their minds set on what the Spirit desires.

Romans 13:14 – Rather, clothe yourselves with the Lord Jesus Christ [Divine Love], and do not think about how to gratify the desires of the sinful nature.

Galatians 5:16-17, 24 – So I say, live by the Spirit [Divine Love], and you will *not gratify the desires of the sinful nature.* For the sinful nature desires what is contrary to the Spirit, and the Spirit what is contrary to the sinful nature. They are in conflict with each other, so that you do not do what you want. Those who belong to Christ Jesus have crucified the sinful nature with its passions and desires.

Ephesians 4:22-24 – You were taught, with regard to your former way of life, to *put off your old self, which is being corrupted by its deceitful desires*; to be made new in the attitude of your minds; and to put on the new self, a created to be like God in true righteousness and holiness.

Colossians 3:5 – Put to death, therefore, whatever belongs to your earthly nature: sexual immorality, impurity, lust, evil desires and greed, which is idolatry.

James 1:14-15 – Each one is tempted when, by his own evil desire, he is dragged away and enticed. Then, after desire has conceived, it gives birth to sin; and sin, when it is full-grown, gives birth to death.

1 Peter 1:14 – As obedient children, do not conform to the evil desires you had when you lived in ignorance [before understanding and receiving the Divine Love].

1 Peter 2:11 – Dear friends, I urge you, as aliens and strangers in the world, to abstain from sinful desires, which war against your soul.

1 John 2:17 – The world and its desires pass away [sin will eventually be eradicated from the universe], but the man who does the will of God [in accepting His Divine Love] lives forever [because he possesses immortality].

Acquiring of Virtues

As our desires change and as we more and more follow spiritual desires, we grow in virtues. Through the New Birth – Divine Love flowing into our souls – we come into a right relationship with God, the ultimate goal of which is at-onement through complete soul transformation, or rebirth of the soul.

A person who is born again/anew will have the external evidences of a good life because they are motivated by God's Love from within. That doesn't mean that they will never sin or succumb to temptation. But as they become more aware of their desires and follow those that spring from the Divine Love within, their life will be more and more virtuous, kind and loving, as well as manifesting the "fruit of the Spirit" listed in Galatians 5 and the virtues listed in 2 Peter 1.

Galatians 5:22-23 – But the fruit of the Spirit is love, joy, peace, patience, kindness, goodness, faithfulness, gentleness and self-control. Against such things there is no law.

2 Peter 1:5-8 – For this very reason, *make every effort* to add to your faith goodness; and to goodness, knowledge; and to knowledge, self-control; and to self-control, perseverance; and to perseverance, godliness; and to godliness, brotherly kindness; and to brotherly kindness, love. For if you possess these qualities in increasing measure, *they will keep you from being ineffective and unproductive* in your knowledge of our Lord Jesus Christ.

To sum up, as we continuously choose to follow the inner guidance of the Divine Love, our desires for material things will diminish as our priorities change. Instead, spiritual pursuits will be gain in importance. We will also be motivated to act in love and kindness, experience faith and peace, and grow in self-control. All this will not happen automatically, however. Our free will needs to be exercised and right choices consciously made. As more of our soul is transformed, loving choices will become more and more second nature.

Chapter 8 – Transformed by Love to Love

The crux of the revelations given to James Padgett is to pray for the Divine Love. Specifically, James was advised: "Your praying must be more frequent so that the soul may be freed from ... thoughts not spiritual. ... You need not wait for occasions or opportunities to formally pray but *all during the day and evening let your longings for the love ascend to the Father*. A long prayer, or even one formulated into words, is not necessary, as [words are not necessary] to give [the longing] form. The longing may be rapid as unformed thought, and as effective for the Father to catch. ... The longing is quicker than the thought, and the answer ... will come with as much certainty and love as if you were to put the longing into the most exact form. Prayers of this kind ascend to the Father and are heard and answered." (TGRABJ/1/5.)

The Bible, often using the term "Holy Spirit" to mean the Divine Love, says in the gospel of Luke:

Luke 11:13 – "If you then, though you are evil, know how to give good gifts to your children, *how much more will your Father in heaven give the Holy Spirit to those who ask him!*"

This chapter shows how the more that we pray and seek God's Love for the transformation of our soul, the more we will be able to live from the soul / spiritual mind and make loving decisions.

It is indeed love – fulfilling what can be regarded as the "Eleventh Commandment" – that transcends the law and identifies us as Jesus' disciples. As the first to inherit the Celestial Kingdom of God, Jesus is the Master of that realm. He is the pioneer of many who have already entered, or are yet to enter, the Father's Kingdom as divine angels transformed by the Divine Love into new creatures and true children of God – immortal as God is immortal. Jesus told his disciples shortly before his death:

John 13:34-35 – *"A new command I give you: Love one another.* As I have loved you [with the Divine Love], so you must love one another. *By this all men will know that you are my disciples, if you love one another."*

He elaborated further:

John 15:8-12 – "This is to my Father's glory, that you *bear much fruit*, showing yourselves to be my disciples. As the Father has loved me, so have I loved you. Now *remain in my love* [Divine Love]. If you obey my commands [to love one another], you will remain in my love, just as I have obeyed my Father's commands and remain in his love. I have told you this so that my joy may be in you and that your joy may be complete. My command is this: *Love each other as I have loved you.* Greater love has no one than this, that he lay down his life for his friends [not necessarily in sacrifice]. You are my friends if you do what I command.

I no longer call you servants, because a servant does not know his master's business. Instead, I have called you friends, for everything that I learned from my Father I have made known to you [the gospel of salvation through Divine Love].

As shown in the previous chapter, desires are the key to and seeds of our actions and their consequences. If our desires are motivated by love, we'll do well and reap blessings, but if they are motivated by the "sinful nature", including ego, the desires will come to fruition as sin.

Romans 8:5-7 tells us: "Those who live according to the sinful nature have their minds set on what that nature desires; but those who live in accordance with the Spirit [Divine Love] have their minds set on what the Spirit desires [spiritual pursuits and loving actions]. The mind of sinful man is death [making the soul dead or dormant], but the mind controlled by the Spirit is life and peace [Divine Love leading to immortality and peace that passes all understanding]; the sinful mind is hostile to God. It does not submit to God's law, nor can it do so."

James sums it up succinctly:

James 1:14-15 – But each one is tempted when, by his own evil desire, he is dragged away and enticed. Then, after desire has conceived, it gives birth to sin; and sin, when it is full-grown, gives birth to death [death of the soul without the Divine Love].

As mentioned, ultimately the Law of Love is the highest law. Love fulfills all individual laws and indeed transcends those laws. In other words, if we love others, motivated by the Divine Love in our souls, we don't have to worry about the minute laws that the Pharisees were in Jesus' time and some Christians still are so particular about – sometimes at the cost of being unloving. We are exhorted in the book of Romans:

Romans 13:8-10 – "Let no debt remain outstanding, except *the continuing debt to love one another, for he who loves his fellowman has fulfilled the law.* The commandments, 'Do not commit adultery,' 'Do not murder' 'Do not steal,' 'Do not covet,' and *whatever other commandment there may be, are summed up in this one rule: 'Love your neighbor as yourself.' Love does no harm to its neighbor. Therefore love is the fulfillment of the law.*"

James 2:8 calls the second great commandment the "royal law". It says: "If you really keep the royal law found in Scripture, 'Love your neighbor as yourself,' you are doing right."

1 Thessalonians 4:9 reads: "Now about brotherly love we do not need to write to you, for *you yourselves have been taught by God* [through His Love working in and changing our hearts and souls] *to love each other.*" (See also John 6:45 and Isaiah 54:13)

Jesus' closest disciple, John, who understood his teaching better than the others, penned these words:

1 John 4:12-18 – No one has ever seen God; but *if we love one another, God lives in us and his love is made complete in us. We know that we live in him and he in us, because he has given us of his Spirit.* [Divine Love imparted by his Holy Spirit]. And we have seen and testify that the Father has sent his son to be the Savior of the world. If anyone acknowledges that Jesus is the son of God [through union with God as a result of the Divine Love], God lives in him and he in God [in the same way that this was true of Jesus]. And so we know and rely on the love God has for us. *God is love. Whoever lives in [Divine] love lives in God, and God in him.* In this way, love is made complete among us so that we will have confidence on the day of judgment [since the law of compensation has been transcended], because in this world we are like him. There is no fear in love. But perfect love drives out fear, because fear has to do with punishment. The one who fears is not made perfect in love.

To finish this chapter, here is a quote from the famous Love chapter in 1 Corinthians 13. Amazingly, spiritual gifts, understanding of mysteries, faith, extreme generosity, and even martyrdom amount to nothing if not motivated by love.

1 Corinthians 13:1-13 – And now I will show you the most excellent way. If I speak in the tongues of men and of angels, but have not love, I am only a resounding gong or a clanging cymbal. If I have the gift of prophecy and can fathom all mysteries and all knowledge, and if I have a faith that can move mountains, but have not love, I am nothing. If I give all I possess to the poor and surrender my body to the flames, but have not love, I gain nothing.

Love is patient, love is kind. It does not envy, it does not boast, it is not proud. It is not rude, it is not self-seeking, it is not easily angered, it keeps no record of wrongs. Love does not delight in evil but rejoices with the truth. It always protects, always trusts, always hopes, always perseveres. Love never fails.

But where there are prophecies, they will cease; where there are tongues, they will be stilled; where there is knowledge, it will pass away. For we know in part and we prophesy in part, but when perfection comes, the imperfect disappears. ... Now we see but a poor reflection as in a mirror; then we shall see face to face. Now I know in part; then I shall know fully, even as I am fully known. And now these three remain: faith, hope and love. But the greatest of these is love.

So to sum up, love – indeed Divine Love – is the most excellent way and the highest law – transcending even the law of compensation. Dwelling in our heart/soul, it transforms us from inside out into loving individuals. Our destiny is to become divine, immortal angels of God who will have unlimited growth potential, understand more and more of divine mysteries, and forever enjoy the beauties of God's Celestial Kingdom. And the best news is that the Divine Love is freely available for the asking.

Chapter 9 – Growth in Spiritual Understanding

The physical mind is limited in its abilities – it simply is not equipped to grasp things of deep spiritual nature. We read in TGRABJ/2/200, "You *cannot perceive spiritual things with the material mind*, neither can a man by reason of those powers of the mind which know only material things, be able to perceive the truths of the spirit. Hence *the necessity for man cultivating the soul perceptions*, which are greater and more comprehending than all the faculties of the material mind."

The Bible concurs and puts it in these words:

1 Corinthians 2:12-14 – We have not received the spirit of the world but the *Spirit who is from God, that we may understand what God has freely given us*. This is what we speak, not in words taught us by human wisdom but in *words taught by the Spirit, expressing spiritual truths in spiritual words*. The man without the Spirit does not accept the things that come from the Spirit of God, for they are foolishness to him, and he cannot understand them, because they are spiritually discerned.

This chapter discusses the difference between the natural mind and the soul mind in terms of receiving understanding.

Importance of Cultivating Soul Perceptions

We learn further from TGRABJ/2/200 (paraphrased) that the mind is indeed a wonderful instrument for investigating the laws of nature and the relationship of cause and effect in the physical world. However, its powers are limited when applied to things of the spirit. The use of the mind in that way can lead to incorrect conclusions, as well as retarding the soul's development of its faculties.

God has created laws to be applied to conditions of both the material world and the spiritual world. But the laws that apply to the operations of the material world may not apply to the operations of the spiritual world. Knowledge of the laws pertaining to the natural will not automatically supply knowledge of the laws pertaining to the spiritual. So to spiritually progress, humans need to become acquainted with the relevant spiritual laws.

The soul is to the spiritual things of God what the mind is to the material things of God. Therefore, it is a mistake to attempt to learn spiritual things through the powers of the material mind. Rather, it is *necessary to exercise the soul perceptions which will come as one's soul develops.* These perceptions are just as real as the five senses of the mind, though most people are not aware of them. Once their existence is understood and they begin to be exercised, the development of these soul faculties or perceptions will progress with success and certainty.

From Truth Discovery to Faith

In TGRABJ/2/337, we learn of a process that leads from the revelation of truth to the development of faith. When a discovered or revealed *truth* is recognized as reality based on experience, it is then put into *action*. This leads to *belief of the mind*, which in turn leads to *faith with longings and aspirations at the soul level*. The object of faith becomes real (of substance) which then leads to *knowledge with conviction*, and as a result, one can speak with authority as Jesus did. Such was the process by which Jesus became the possessor and authentic expositor of the great spiritual truths that had never before been known and declared by any person.

These steps leading to knowledge and internalization of truth must be followed gradually and with confidence. The help and influence of the Father are necessary in this, and come only in response to sincere prayer from the soul. This is the only means to obtain deep spiritual knowledge – it is always by grace. All knowledge of spiritual things coming in any other way cannot be relied on, for there is only one source of such knowledge out of which the real spiritual truths of God emanate.

In sum, naturally, through the human mind, it is impossible to understand spiritual things or arrive at correct conclusions regarding spirit matters. The higher spiritual truths can only be grasped through soul perceptions or the soul-mind. As one receives more of the Divine Love through the Holy Spirit, the individual becomes aware of their soul faculties which will further develop as more of the Divine Love finds lodgement in the soul. The development of soul perceptions results in a deeper understanding of the higher spiritual truths and our relationship with God.

Chapter 10 – Born of Water and the Spirit

In John 3:5-7, Jesus told Nicodemus: "I tell you the truth, no one can enter the kingdom of God unless he is *born of water and the Spirit*. Flesh gives birth to flesh, but the *Spirit gives birth to spirit*. You should not be surprised at my saying, 'You must be born again.'"

As mentioned, Jesus' teaching about the New Birth was that God's Divine Love, withdrawn from humankind with the fall of the first parents, had been re-bestowed by the Father in His goodness and mercy. Jesus, having his soul filled with the Father's Love imparted by the Holy Spirit, was the visible proof of its bestowal.

This chapter explores the water symbolism as related to the New Birth.

Water of Eternal Life

In another Bible account, Jesus spoke to a Samaritan woman at a well about "living water" he had to give and the type of worship the Father desires.

John 4:10-15, 20-24 – Jesus answered her, "If you knew the gift of God and who it is that asks you for a drink, you would have asked him and *he would have given you living water*." "Sir," the woman said, "you have nothing to draw with and the well is deep. Where can you get this living water? Are you greater than our father Jacob, who gave us the well and drank from it himself, as did also his sons and his flocks and herds?" Jesus answered, "Everyone who drinks this water will be thirsty again, but whoever drinks the water I give him will never thirst. Indeed, *the water I give him will become in him a spring of water welling up to eternal life.*" The woman said to him, "Sir, give me this water so that I won't get thirsty and have to keep coming here to draw water." ... "Our fathers worshiped on this mountain, but you Jews claim that the place where we must worship is in Jerusalem." Jesus declared, "Believe me, woman, a time is coming when you will worship the Father neither on this mountain nor in Jerusalem. ... A time is coming and has now come when the *true worshipers will worship the Father in spirit and truth*, for they are the kind of worshipers the Father seeks. God is spirit, and his worshipers must worship in spirit and in truth."

The spiritual worship that the Father seeks comes into effect once a person starts asking for the gift of the Holy Spirit/Divine Love – symbolized by living water welling up to eternal life. Such worship includes spending time in prayer (verbal, silent and/or meditation), fellowshipping with God and fellow believers, as well as spiritual reading.

As we spend time with the Father, we can experience not only peace and love, but may find answers to situations or problems deposited into our souls as we sit in silence after praying. Insights for life and spiritual growth may also come at other times and in different ways if our souls are receptive and attuned to the guidance and promptings of righteous spirits and Celestial angels. This too, in the broader sense, would be worship in spirit.

Another clue about the life-giving spiritual water can be found in the book of Titus.

Titus 3:3-7 – At one time we too were foolish, disobedient, deceived and enslaved by all kinds of passions and pleasures. We lived in malice and envy, being hated and hating one another. But when the kindness and love of God our Savior appeared [the time of re-bestowal of the Divine Love], he saved us, not because of righteous things we had done, but because of his mercy. He *saved us through the washing of rebirth and renewal by the Holy Spirit*, whom he poured out on us generously through [the teachings of] Jesus Christ our Savior, so that, having been *justified by his grace*, we might become heirs *having the hope of eternal life.*

So again, the Holy Spirit, imparting the Divine Love, is symbolized by "living water" – the agent of washing, renewal, and eventually eternal life and immortality in the Celestial Kingdom.

Water of Divine Truth

Further, in the gospel of John, we learn that *Jesus' teachings are spirit and life*. Other passages show them to have, like water, a cleansing and purifying effect.

John 6:63 – The Spirit gives life; the flesh counts for nothing. The *words I have spoken to you are spirit and they are life.*

Ephesians 5:26 – ... to make [the church] holy, cleansing her by the *washing with water through the word.*

John 15:3 – You are already *clean because of the word I [Jesus] have spoken to you.*

John 17:17 – *Sanctify them* [make them holy, set them apart] *by the truth;* your word is truth.

Reborn through God's Word of Truth

Jesus' God-given message that the Divine Love was again available to humanity was the life-giving truth that if acted on, would indeed lead to eternal life. Imparted through the Holy Spirit into one's soul, the Divine Love would be a cleansing and purifying agent, eradicating sin and error. It would also be transforming the soul from a divine image into divine substance, giving it immortality. This process is what it means to be born again – to experience the New Birth. Several Bible passages confirm this truth, for example:

1 Peter 1:22-23 – Now that you have *purified yourselves by obeying the truth* so that you have sincere love for your brothers, love one another deeply, from the heart. For you have been *born again, not of perishable seed, but of imperishable, through the living and enduring word of God.*

James 1:18 – He chose to *give us birth through the word of truth*, that we might be a kind of firstfruits of all he created.

John 1:12-13 – Yet to all who received him, to those who believed in his name [as the Savior bringing life-giving teachings], he gave the *right to become children of God* – children born not of natural descent, nor of human decision or a husband's will, *but born of God.*

So to sum up, the water is not merely a symbol of purification, but represents the "living waters" of God's own essence, His Divine Love, which fills the soul and enables it to live. The Holy Spirit does not come to dwell in a human soul but, as the instrument of God, conveys the Father's Love into the soul of the earnest seeker. God's Word, brought to humanity by Jesus, about the Divine Love again becoming available, is spirit and the key to the New Birth. This transformation of a human soul into a divine soul, and the consequent purification from sin qualifies the soul to live throughout all eternity with God in His Celestial mansions. This is the Love which Jesus manifested in his soul and with which his apostles were to love one another.

Jesus was the first human born from above – born of the Holy Spirit in that it is the agent through which the Father's Love was poured out in abundance into his soul. And he told Nicodemus that he, as well as all who would obey his life-giving spirit teachings, could also be reborn through the Spirit and become at-one with the Father.

Chapter 11 – Saved by Grace through Faith

As mentioned earlier, salvation comes by God's grace through soul transformation by the Divine Love. However, the soul has to be opened in order to be receptive to the inflowing of the Love imparted by the Holy Spirit. In the book of Ephesians, we read:

Ephesians 2:8-9 – For it is *by grace you have been saved, through faith* – and this not from yourselves, *it is the gift of God* — *not by works, so that no one can boast.*

Our pre-salvation state was one of "being dead in transgressions and sins, following the ways of this world, and gratifying the cravings of our sinful nature and following its desires and thoughts" (Ephesians 2:1-3). But we read in the following three verses (4-6): "Because of *his great love for us*, God, who is rich in mercy, *made us alive with Christ* even when we were dead in transgressions —it is *by grace you have been saved.* And God raised us up with Christ and *seated us with him in the heavenly realms in Christ Jesus.*"

By grace, we were raised from our dead soul state through the Divine Love, given immortality, and eventually we'll occupy the Celestial heavenly realms, where Jesus is the firstborn of many brethren and the loving and benevolent Master. This chapter explores where faith fits into the equation. Faith can mean several things, but true faith is more than just mental belief. The various aspects of faith will now be discussed.

Faith as a Point in Time

The New Testament in the book of Galatians mentions circumstances "before faith" and "after faith has come", and contrasts living by faith with keeping the law. These points in time can occur on a global or individual level.

Globally the time of faith starts with Jesus' coming and his announcement about the re-availability of the Divine Love. Before that, moral (as well as some ceremonial) laws were to guide human behavior. However, as history and the Old Testament show, these God-given laws were often disobeyed, which brought about unpleasant consequences. The law of cause and effect or the law of compensation was in full operation both on earth and in the spirit world. But when Jesus announced the re-bestowal of the Divine Love, not everyone was ready to accept the Good News – in fact most were not.

We learn from TGRABJ/3/303 that "the teachings of the Master were twofold, and for those who were not in a condition to hear and understand his higher spiritual truths, he preached those things, which if followed, would make them better men and women and cause them to progress in the development of their natural love." Paraphrasing what follows, natural love teachings and the work of preachers and teachers who have limited understanding must therefore not be undervalued, for people differ in their intellectual and spiritual conditions. The truths taught may by their influence on the hearts of the hearers turn their minds to spiritual things of the higher nature. This then may open their souls to the influence of Celestial spirits, and from that may follow longings for the Love of the Father.

On an individual level, the time of faith has to do with one's spiritual development. This determines a person's readiness to accept Jesus' invitation to take on his light yoke and embark on the path of faith, grace and Divine Love, as contrasted with the more difficult natural love pathway of striving to keep the law and overcoming one's weakness on one's own strength.

The passage in Galatians 3:23 to 4:7 gives us insights on our position before and after embarking on the Divine Love path, or, as the scripture calls it, the path of faith. In verses 23 and 24, Paul explains the role of the law, or moral teachings: it was a temporary "tutor" before we were ready to follow the path of the Divine Love and faith. The passage then moves on and tells us what happened when "faith" came:

Galatians 3:23-26 – But *before faith [Divine Love teaching] came,* we were kept under guard by the law, kept for the faith which would afterward be revealed. Therefore the law was our tutor to bring us to Christ [Divine Love], that we might be *justified by faith*. But *after faith has come,* we are no longer under a tutor. *For you are all sons of God through faith in Christ Jesus.* So the law was put in charge to lead us to Christ that we might be justified by faith. *Now that faith has come, we are no longer under the supervision of the law."*

Chapter 4 of Galatians then continues and concludes:

Galatians 4:1-7 – What I am saying is that as long as the heir is a child, he is no different from a slave, although he owns the whole estate. He is subject to guardians and trustees until the time set by his father. So also, when we were children [spiritually immature], we were in slavery under the basic principles of the world. But *when the time had fully come, God sent his Son*, born of a woman, born under law, *to redeem those under law* [redeem them from experiencing the law of compensation which every breaking of the law automatically brings], that we might receive the full rights of sons. Because you are sons [begotten of God and God's true children], God sent the Spirit of his Son into our hearts [Divine Love, which was first in Jesus' soul], the Spirit who calls out, "Abba, Father." So you are no longer a slave [to the law], but a son; and since you are a son, God has made you also an heir [heir to God's Kingdom through the Divine Love].

So in this context, faith is the time when Jesus brought God's saving knowledge about the Divine Love to the world, or when we individually become ready to receive and act on this information.

The Development and Object of Faith

In TGRABJ/2/337, we read of a process that leads to the development of faith. When a discovered or revealed truth is recognized as reality, it is put into action. This leads to belief of the mind, which in turn leads to *faith with longings and aspirations at the soul level*. The object of faith becomes real (of substance) which then leads to knowledge with conviction, and as a result, one can speak with authority as Jesus did.

The truth needed for salvation is what Jesus came to reveal and live, and God's promises associated therewith. This is the teaching of the New Birth through Divine Love flowing into and transforming one's soul. Of and by ourselves, we are not divine or immortal. Having sinned, we are subject to the law of compensation (in Bible terminology, judgment) which in the spirit world may involve considerable suffering before this law is satisfied. The law of Love transcends the law of compensation. If we believe and accept Jesus' teaching, realize and admit our helplessness and sinfulness, and come to God, we are unconditionally and by grace promised the gift of the Divine Love.

TGRABJ/1/20, paraphrased, tells us that when individuals *believe with all the sincerity of their minds and souls* that the Love of the Father is waiting and available to each of them for the asking, and when they *come to the Father in faith and earnest aspiration,* this love will not be withheld from them. If, in addition to this belief, they *pray with all the earnestness and longings of their souls* that God open up their souls to the inflowing of this Love, the Holy Spirit will bring the Love into their souls in abundance. The person who will thus *believe and pray* will never be disappointed, and the way to the kingdom is guaranteed to be theirs. There is no need for a mediator, or prayers or ceremonies of priests and preachers. God Himself hears man's prayers and personally responds by sending the Comforter – the Holy Spirit.

As more and more Divine Love is received in response to earnest prayer, faith increases proportionately. With this, the object of faith, the Love in the soul, becomes a perceived reality. So the more one prays, the more Love and faith is given, and the more awareness of the Love – the Love and its associated attributes become a felt substance and an object of knowledge. (Cf. Hebrews 11: 1.)

The Prayer Perfect (found in TGRABJ/1/40 as well as later in this book) tells us to ask: *"that there may come to us faith – such faith as will cause us to realize that we are truly Your children and one with You in very substance and not in image only."* As the Divine Love transforms our souls, its emanating illumination assures us of its reality. The soul is no longer just an image of God, the Great Soul, but is becoming filled with the substance of the Father's essence.

The Prayer goes on to say: "Let us have such *faith as will cause us to know* that You are our Father, and the bestower of every good and perfect gift and that only we, ourselves, can prevent Your love changing us from the mortal to the immortal."

As discussed in an earlier chapter, the Bible confirms that we become God's children in the same way that Jesus was the first son of the Father – through having God's substance, His Love, abide in and transform his soul. If we believe Jesus' teaching about the Divine Love and put it into action by praying for the Love, we are promised tangible results (substance), which will in turn increase our faith that the teaching is true. Further application of the teaching and growth in the Love will result in growth in faith. In a passage in John's gospel, we read:

John 1:12-13 – Yet to all who received [Jesus], to those who *believed* in his name [his special mission as God's messenger and his teachings], he gave *the right to become children of God* – children born not of natural descent, nor of human decision or a husband's will, but *born of God.*

Furthermore:

Romans 8:14-17 – Those who are led by the Spirit of God [Divine Love] are sons of God. For you did not receive a spirit that makes you a slave again to fear, but you received the Spirit of sonship. And by him we cry, "Abba, Father." *The Spirit himself testifies with our spirit that we are God's children.* Now if we are children, then we are heirs – heirs of God and co-heirs with Christ, if indeed we share in his sufferings in order that we may also share in his glory. (See also Galatians 3:26 and 4:5, as well as Ephesians 1:5)

The key is believing in Jesus, and, even more importantly, accepting and acting on his teachings.

1 John 3:23-24 – And this is [God's] command: to believe in the name of his Son, Jesus Christ, and to love one another as [Jesus] commanded us. Those who obey [God's] commands live in him, and he in them. And this is how we know that he lives in us: *We know it by the Spirit he gave us* [which imparts Divine Love].

1 John 4:13-18 – We know that we live in [God] and he in us, because he has given us of his Spirit [which imparts the Divine Love]. And we have seen and testify that the Father has sent his Son to be the Savior of the world [by revealing and living the way of salvation and immortality through the Divine Love]. If anyone acknowledges that Jesus is the Son of God [through the Divine Love transforming his soul], *God lives in him and he in God*. And so we know and rely on the love God has for us. God is love. *Whoever lives in love lives in God, and God in him*. In this way, love is made complete among us so that we will have confidence on the day of judgment [since the law of compensation will be transcended], because in this world we are like him. There is no fear in love. But perfect love drives out fear, because fear has to do with punishment. The one who fears is not made perfect in love.

Effects of Faith

Here are further tips on growing in faith and the effects thereof. Quoting from TGRABJ/2/137: "Let the love in you increase and pray to the Father for more faith in His promises, and for a greater inflowing of His Love. Very soon *you will realize His actual presence in your soul to an extent that will make you know that you are one with him in Love, and in the possession of the divine essence. This will cause all doubt to leave you*, and give you a faith in which no doubt will appear."

Paraphrasing from TGRABJ/2/132, we get a few more insights: You must *pray for more faith and trust implicitly in His promises, and in the promises of the Master,* for they will be fulfilled and you will not be disappointed or left to yourself. Your soul must be developed with this Divine Love of the Father. Soul development in Divine Love goes hand-in-hand with *earnest, sincere prayer to the Father*. With such prayer will come faith, and with faith will come the substance of what you may now only believe. So *pray often, believing that the Love of the Father will come to you, and you will realize your oneness with Him. Let not the things of the world distract your attention from these spiritual necessities*, and *you will find that all these material things will be supplied you*. Be firm and courageous in your beliefs, and God will be with you in every hour of trial and distress. Let your faith increase until doubt shall flee away, and only trust in the Love and goodness of God remain with you.

In another message focusing on faith, TGRABJ/1/209, Jesus tells us (paraphrased): If you will earnestly seek God's Love, you will find that there will come to you such *a belief in His wonderful Love and in the nearness of His presence, that you will be free from all doubt.*

Faith is not the belief that arises from the operation of the mind, but rather comes from the opening of the perceptions of the soul. Faith is greater than belief, and exists in its true sense only in the soul. Belief may arise from a conviction of the mind, but faith never can. No one can possess it unless his soul is awakened by the inflowing of the Love. Faith is based on the possession of this Love, and without it there can be no faith.

Faith is a progressive quality or essence of the soul, and increases as possession of the Divine Love increases. It is not dependent on anything else. Prayers for Divine Love call from the Father a response that brings with it faith, and *with this faith comes a knowledge of the existence of this Love in your own soul.* So when we pray to the Father to increase our faith, it is a prayer for the increase of Love.

True faith *makes the aspirations and longings of the soul a real, living existence. It enables its possessor to "see" God in all His beauty and Love.* This means that the person's soul perceptions will be in such condition that the *Father's attributes will appear plainly to him.*

We read further in TGRABJ/2/131 (paraphrased): The faith that you must try to obtain *will transcend all the worries and troubles that may come to you. This kind of faith overcomes every obstacle, and makes you a true child of the Father and one whom He will never forsake or let go unprovided for.*

The Bible confirms that true faith is conditional on the Love in the soul. In Galatians 5:6 we read, "For in Christ Jesus neither circumcision nor uncircumcision has any value. The only thing that counts is *faith expressing itself through love.*" According to Mark Kramer, in Greek, the phrase "expressing itself" (translated from *energeo*) means *"to be operative, be at work."* So, literally, Galatians 5:6 says, "… faith, being operative by the Divine Love (*agape*)."

Faith comes only with constant earnest prayer. As Jesus states in TGRABJ/1/209, "Your prayers call from the Father a response that brings with it faith, and with this faith comes a knowledge of the existence of this Love in your own soul." The writer in the book of Hebrews echoes this:

Hebrews 11:1 – "Now faith is being sure of what we hope for and certain of what we do not see." (NIV translation) or "Now faith is the substance of things hoped for, the evidence of things not seen." (KJV) In the original Greek text, the word *hupostasis* is used for "substance", meaning: "that which has actual existence; a substance, a real thing."

So faith, the amount of which is proportional to the Divine Love in one's soul, gives us firm knowledge and conviction that the Love is real – of substance – and that we are true children of God. Faith further helps us to transcend our worries and concerns, gives us confidence in trials and assures us that God's promises will come to pass.

Faith Transcends Wrong Beliefs

We are also taught that many who haven't specifically heard of Jesus or been exposed to the truth of the Divine Love, or those who have wrong beliefs about salvation, may at the soul level be desiring and receiving God's Love and be transformed by it. For example, in TGRABJ/2/136, a message from Jesus tells us: "I know that the people who were worshipping me were not doing what I approve of or like, but their hearts were turned to God; and while they were making me the object of their worship, yet the spirit of God was with them, and the workings of the Holy Spirit were in the hearts of very many of them showing them the Love of the Father and the truth of His salvation. They, of course, are mistaken when they talk about being saved by my blood, for my blood has nothing to do with their salvation ... But, *notwithstanding this false belief, these people in their prayers actually aspire for the Love of God, and He knows the longings of their hearts and sends the Holy [Spirit] to fill them with this Divine Love* which makes them become very close to the Father, and makes them happy."

Many people of other than the Christian faith have rich spiritual understanding and may well be receiving the Divine Love at the soul level, and be true children of God and on the way to the Celestial Heavens. Therefore, no one is in the position to judge another as to their soul condition, much less their spiritual destiny.

So to sum up, belief in and application of Jesus' teachings will result in the receiving of the Divine Love in our souls. With more Love will in turn come more faith, and true faith, arising from the soul, will eliminate doubts and transcend worries. There will be a certainty in knowing that we are truly God's children, that God is our loving Father, that His Love is transforming our souls and making us at one with Him and immortal, that He is with us and close to us, that He will provide for all our earthly needs and help us overcome obstacles, and that our destiny in His Celestial Kingdom is assured.

Part III – Entering Divine Glory

Part III deals with the final aspect of our salvation process – reaching a state of glorification in the Celestial Kingdom of God. This is when a person has achieved a full transformation of their soul from the image of God into the substance of the Father. They are not just perfect and sinless, but also immortal. This state is possible to reach in the physical life, but few do. We know that Jesus accomplished this. Being the first to receive the Divine Love and reach the state of full New Birth, he has become our forerunner, example, and pioneer of our salvation. He and other Celestial spirits – divine angels in the Father's Kingdom – are influencing, guiding and assisting mortals and spirits to help them fulfil their ultimate potential and divine destiny.

Chapter 12 gives glimpses of life in the Celestial Kingdom – time of unlimited possibility of growth and service, unimaginable beauty, and unsurpassed and ever-increasing happiness.

Chapter 12 – Celestial Kingdom of God

When our souls are fully transformed from the image of God into divine substance, the spiritual gestation period ends and the full birth as children of God / divine angels will have taken place. Those who have reached this state are qualified to enter the Celestial Heavens – a glorified existence of unlimited potential where Jesus is the Master. This chapter gives glimpses of the life and work of the inhabitants of the Kingdom of God.

Children of God, But Not Equal to God

As shown in Chapter 3, we are God's true children as soon as we start receiving the Divine Love, in the same way that an embryo or fetus is already a child of its parents. We read in the first letter of John:

1 John 3:1-2 – How great is the love the Father has lavished on us, that we should be called children of God! And that is what we are! The reason the world does not know us is that it did not know him. Dear friends, *now we are children of God*, and what we will be has not yet been made known. But we know that when he appears, *we shall be like him, for we shall see him as he is* [in the Celestial Kingdom through soul perceptions].

We also read in Paul's first letter to the Corinthians:

1 Corinthians 13:12 – Now we see but a poor reflection as in a mirror; then we shall see face to face. *Now I know in part; then I shall know fully, even as I am fully known.*

So while in the physical body, our knowledge and experience of God is limited, though it increases as we grow in the Divine Love and with it in soul perceptions. At death, we will shed the bodies of flesh and retain our spirit bodies. Their brightness or otherwise will correspond to our soul condition. The more our soul is developed in the Divine Love, the more glorious our spirit body. Even when our soul transformation is complete, there will be no limit to our growth in the Divine Love and corresponding glory.

As children of God, we are also brothers and sisters of Jesus Christ (Hebrews 2:11-12). He is the pioneer of our salvation and the first to have reached the Celestial Kingdom, whereof he is the Master. He is the most developed spirit in the Divine Love and closest to the fountainhead of God.

While our transformed souls become one in essence with the Love of the Great Soul, it does not mean that we become God as the Father is God. It does mean that the quality of Love possessed by our transformed souls is such that we will never experience death. We will not receive all of God's attributes, such as omniscience and omnipotence. This way the Father will always remain the one and only God. Even Jesus is not God, but only one, and the first, of God's children in the divine sense, with many to follow.

From TGRABJ/2/320, paraphrased, we learn regarding our ultimate status in relation to God: All partake of God's Divine Being – his attributes – but there is a difference in the workings and scope of the operations of the various divine attributes. *The divine is that which has in it, to a sufficient degree, the very substance and essence of God Himself.* Divinity belongs to God alone, and can be possessed by spirits or mortals only when He has transfused into their souls a portion of this divinity, and to that extent made them a part of Himself. Nothing in the universe is divine or partakes of the divine except that which is of the soul, for all else is of the material, and this even when it has the form or appearance of the spirit. *Even the soul, as created, is not divine and cannot become such, until it is transformed into the divine by the transfusion into it of divine substance.* Many souls in the spirit world, although pure and in harmony with their created condition, are not divine. They cannot become such because they do not desire and seek divinity in the only way provided by the Father.

God's creations are no more a part of God or divine than human creations are a part of their creator or human. God is wholly divine as are all His attributes – which may be separated in their workings and bestowals. The person or soul that is the recipient of one of God's qualities is not necessarily the recipient of the others.

Omnipotence and omniscience are never given to humans or spirits – God remains their exclusive possessor, although in all His attributes there are powers and knowledge. While humans may receive one of the divine attributes, *this does not make them Deity*. There is and can be only one God, although He may give of His essence and substance, so that an individual can become as He is in that essence and substance, to the extent that it is bestowed.

As regards human salvation and happiness, the greatest of God's attributes is His Divine Love, which is the only one that can bring the souls of humans into a oneness in nature with the Father, and which contains the quality of immortality. This Love has a transforming power and can change something of a different substance into the same essence as itself. In addition, it can eliminate from that thing its innate, but undesirable components, without injuring or destroying the thing itself.

Glimpse of the Glorified State

To give three of his disciples a foretaste of the glorified Celestial Kingdom existence, Jesus arranged for the transfiguration vision. We read about it in all three of the synoptic gospels, but here is a quote from Matthew:

Matthew 17:1-3 – After six days Jesus took with him Peter, James and John the brother of James, and led them up a high mountain by themselves. There he was transfigured before them. *His face shone like the sun, and his clothes became as white as the light.* Just then there appeared before them Moses and Elijah, talking with Jesus.

Elijah comments later in TGRABJ/1/271: "At the time of the transfiguration on the mount, some of us possessed that Love to such a degree that our appearances were shining and bright, as described in the Bible. But Jesus was brighter than Moses or myself, for he had more of this Divine Love in his soul and could manifest it to the wonderful degree that he did, notwithstanding his physical body."

Life in the Celestial Kingdom

We are given a few glimpses of the beauty and happiness in the Celestial Kingdom of God in TGRABJ/2/60 and 3/268, where Ann Rollins shares (paraphrased): I am now in the Second Celestial Sphere, where everything is so beautiful, and happiness exists to a degree that I cannot portray to you. I am in my own home. It is not possible for me to describe its appearance, only to say that its beauty is beyond any conception that you may have. It has everything that the heart may wish for and everything that you can conceive of as necessary to make a home beautiful. I am in a great degree of happiness, and have many bright and beautiful spirits for companions. Also, I never get tired of listening to the grand and angelic music.

My home is of a material that you have no counterpart of on earth, and it is furnished with everything that makes me happy and thankful to the Father for His Love and kindness. I am living alone, but have many visitors, and love is the ruling sentiment among all the inhabitants here. No spirit who is not filled with the Divine Love can live in this sphere. Spirits who may have the most wonderful intellectual acquirements, but are without this Love, cannot enter this sphere, nor can the mere natural love of mortals or spirits fit them for inhabitancy here. Only the Divine Love of the Father can make a spirit at-one with the surroundings and atmosphere of love that exists here.

The spirits here are so much more beautiful than those of any other sphere that I have lived in. They are more ethereal and their garments are all shining and white. Nothing here reminds one of the earth or the grosser spheres of the spirit world. And the music here is entirely divine and of such a great variety – all telling of the great Love of God, and sung in His praise and adoration.

TGRABJ/2/261 (paraphrased) gives a few more glimpses of life in the Third Celestial Sphere, as reported by Helen Padgett: I have been praying and trying to get more Love of the Father in my soul and have succeeded to such an extent that I am now in the Third Celestial Sphere. I don't have the words at my command to give you any satisfactory idea of the appearance and conditions here. I have described to you my home in the Second Celestial Sphere, though very inadequately, but that home cannot compare with what I have now. I can only say it is beyond all conception of what you can have of beauty, grandeur and love. I am only in the lower planes of this sphere, but these are so filled with the Father's Love that it almost seems impossible that there can be any spheres where there is more of this Love. But of course, as Jesus and others have their homes in the higher Celestial Spheres and nearer to the fountainhead of Love, there must be yet more Love there.

I am so happy that I can scarcely tell you what this happiness means, but there is never the slightest thing to interfere with my happiness or to make me think that I am not an accepted child of the Father, partaking of His Love to an extent that makes me immortal and never again subject to death. This happiness is not such as satisfies only for a while, but is one continual source of living, free from anything that might take away from being one with the Father and a part of Him in Love and beauty.

Even those who have reached the stage of redemption in the Third Spirit Sphere (below the Celestial Heavens) – a state where their souls are purified and the law of compensation has no more power over them – experience wonderful happiness which increases as they progress through the Fifth and Seventh Sphere to the Celestial Kingdom. Here, based on TGRABJ/3/26, are a few glimpses given by Helen Padgett of her earlier spiritual journey.

Spiritually, I am now in [the Fifth Spirit Sphere] that enables me to know what the Love of God really is, and in this Love I have almost complete happiness. I now love everybody, and am trying my best to help every soul that I possibly can. Feelings of dislike, envy or hatred have no place in my heart, for which I thank God.

My home here is much more beautiful than that which I had in the Third Spirit Sphere, and everything is beyond what I conceived when I lived there. The house, trees, flowers and fruits are very much more beautiful and delightful. No one could be anything but happy in such a home. We have nothing to interfere with our happiness and every one is a delightful companion and full of love and beauty. I have met many spirits that I did not know either on earth or in the spirit world before I came to this place, both men and women.

I am sometimes engaged in painting these flowers and landscapes, and have many pictures which others painted. I find that I can paint with a more artistic touch than when on earth. I am also studying music, and especially enjoy my vocal lessons. Sometimes I try to sing some of the songs that I used to sing to you, but they are not pretty in comparison to the songs we have here, either in the music or the sentiments.

Concluding about her progression and the help she has received along the way, Helen shares further in TGRABJ/1/317: I now have God's Love to a considerable degree, and the more of it I get, the happier I am. I thought that I was happy when I entered the Third Sphere, and more so in the Fifth, and then supremely so in the Seventh, but, really, I did not know what happiness was, until I got into my present home in the Celestial Heavens; and I suppose as I go higher, the happiness of each succeeding sphere will be much greater than that from which I progressed.

But, of course, the Master has been the great teacher, whose love and power have helped me more than all the others. He is so wonderful in love and wisdom that I almost adore him, although he says that I must worship only God, and I follow his directions.

My experiences here are so wonderful that I hardly realize what it all means. My time in the spirit world has been so short, and yet, the wonderful knowledge of spiritual truths and the great happiness that I have received, cause me to wonder in amazement that such things could be. (For more insights see also TGRABJ/2/29.)

Work of Glorified Spirits

As we learned, the divine angels have beautiful homes and enjoy immense happiness. A part of their joy, however, comes from service to others. In TGRABJ/3/251 (paraphrased), we receive a few glimpses.

More of the Celestial spirits are performing missions of love in the earth planes than might be expected, considering the happiness that their homes give them. But these spirits know no selfishness in the sense of desiring all this happiness for themselves. Of course, if they have no attraction on earth – if love for mortals does not call them there – they live mostly in the spirit heavens or Celestial Heavens, but always work for others. Spirits are never idle, indulging their own pleasures in the way that Christians often imagine. They do have their harps and music of various kinds and all those things commonly conceived to exist in the Kingdom of Heaven. However, they enjoy them only in moments of cessation from their work in helping other spirits to progress towards the fountainhead of the Father's Love.

I [Helen] am also now working in teaching the spirits of the lower spheres the plan of God for the salvation of their souls. It is a glorious work, and the resulting happiness is beyond explanation. As we give knowledge and love to these spirits and realize their happiness and joy, more love streams down upon us from the higher planes filling our souls with increased abundance, and we realize the saying, that the more we give, the more we receive. We are never made poor by giving and never cease to give when the opportunity presents itself. We are only disappointed when those to whom we try to give our love and share our happiness with, refuse to receive these gifts. This happens frequently in the lower spheres, and especially in the intellectual spheres, where the divine angels spend much time trying to lead those spirits to the way of the Divine Love and endless progress.

Helen shares elsewhere (TGRABJ/3/20 and 26, paraphrased) about her work when she was in the Third and Fifth Spirit Spheres – below the Celestial Spheres, but on the way there: I am also trying to help the spirits who are in a condition of blindness and doubt. Much of my time is given to helping the spirits who do not know the way to God's Love, and the necessity for obtaining it in order to find perfect happiness. I am also engaged in studying the laws pertaining to spirit communication with mortals. And I am specially endowed with the power to find the soulmates of spirits. Many here have no conception of what a soulmate means. They seem to think that they have to remain all alone, until some day they may meet a spirit to whom they may become attached and live with. But when through my work they find their soulmates, they become ever so much happier.

The Father is so loving and good that he never prevents His spirits in the Celestial Kingdom from indulging in things that make them happy, and so despite occasional disappointments, divine angels and spirits in the higher spheres of the spirit kingdom live in supreme contentment.

Prepared Places

Shortly before his death, according to the gospel of John, Jesus told his disciples:

John 14:2 – "In my Father's house are many rooms ["mansions" in KJV]; if it were not so, I would have told you. I am going there to prepare a place for you.

In TGRABJ/2/34 and 3/43, Jesus further elaborated on the nature of his Father's Kingdom (paraphrased): I meant that in the Kingdom of God there are homes, and that I would go and prepare a place where my followers would have a home with me, separate from the spirits who didn't believe in or follow me. My kingdom was to be a separate kingdom from the other parts of the spirit lands, and those who wanted to live with me would have to get the Love of God in their hearts to do so. I have now completed the preparations and it rests with spirits and mortals only to become inhabitants thereof.

The Divine Love has no counterpart in all the universe. It must be received in its fullness for a person to attain the Celestial Spheres, where the Father's fountainhead of Love exists. No one can become a part of God's divinity until they receive this Divine Love and realize that they are one with the Father in Love and purity.

Those who have received the Divine Love are way beyond the lower spirits in intellectual development and spiritual knowledge. Their soul development has enabled them to obtain great soul perceptions. They don't allow anything to lead them to any actions that would be out of harmony with the Divine Love and God's laws. They are in perfect peace and their happiness is beyond all comparison.

And once more from Helen Padgett (TGRABJ/2/28): "Faith and prayer can open the very heart of the Celestial Spheres, and Love will flow down into your soul as the avalanche of snow that feels the warmth of the sun's bright rays rushes from its mountain heights when winter leaves with its chilling gloom and blasting breath for other climes. Love is not only warmth, but it is the very burnings of the soul's great storehouse of God's divine essence.

I am not only the possessor of this Love to a large degree, but I realize that as I advance to higher spheres there is a greater abundance awaiting to fill my soul with its great undying fires of never ending burnings – but burnings so great and free from everything that makes for unhappiness and discontent."

How amazing is the Celestial Kingdom and what incredible places Jesus has prepared, which will be more than worth all the effort and the trials of this earthly life! The apostle Paul is quoted as saying:

1 Corinthians 2:9-10 – As it is written: "No eye has seen, no ear has heard, no mind has conceived what God has prepared for those who love him", but God has revealed it to us by his Spirit. The Spirit searches all things, even the deep things of God.

Romans 8:18 – I consider that our present sufferings are not worth comparing with the glory that will be revealed in us.

2 Corinthians 4:16-18 – Therefore we do not lose heart. Though outwardly we are wasting away, yet inwardly we are being renewed day by day. For our light and momentary troubles are achieving for us an eternal glory that far outweighs them all. So we fix our eyes not on what is seen, but on what is unseen. For what is seen is temporary, but what is unseen is eternal.

May the hope we have of indescribable beauty and happiness carry us forward to the realization of our incredibly glorious potential which has no bounds or limits. May this hope overshadow all the trials and challenges of the earthly life, which compared with eternity is a mere moment in time. And as we are exhorted, may we make every effort to encourage the work of the Divine Love in our souls here and now, so that the joys of being in our Father's awesome Kingdom can be ours soon after passing over from this life to the next.

Prayers for Divine Love

The following is a prayer given by Jesus for the receipt of the Divine Love. It doesn't have to be prayed verbatim, but it can give ideas how to approach the Father who is always happy when His children ask for His Holy Spirit which imparts the Divine Love (see Luke 11:13).

In effect, the prayer contains the basic truths given to humankind by Celestial Spirits. One person used the following analogy: Praying with these words, thought by thought, is like appreciating the beauty of a crystal chandelier, many little crystals of divine truth that we behold in our meditations, and throughout our day.

This longer, formal prayer can be substituted by personal heartfelt prayers and, as one goes about their daily tasks and becomes aware of God during their day, brief, even non-verbal, requests expressing the soul's desire for the Divine Love can be uttered at any time or place.

The Prayer Perfect

Our Father, who are in heaven, we recognize that You are all holy and loving and merciful, and that we are Your children, and not the subservient, sinful and depraved creatures that our false teachers would have us believe. (Matthew 6:9; 1 John 4:8, 16)

Prayer for Divine Love

That we are the greatest of Your creation, and the most wonderful of all Your handiworks, and the objects of Your great Soul's Love and tenderest care. (Psalm 139:13-18)

That Your will is that we become at one with You, and partake of Your great Love which You have bestowed upon us through Your mercy and desire that we become, in truth, Your children, through Love, and not through the sacrifice and death of any one of Your creatures. (John 17:11, 20-26)

We pray that You will open up our souls to the inflowing of Your Love, and that then may come Your Holy Spirit to bring into our souls this, Your Love in great abundance, until our souls shall be transformed into the very essence of Yourself; and that there may come to us faith – such faith as will cause us to realize that we are truly Your children and one with You in very substance and not in image only. (1 John 4:7, 12-13, 16-17)

Let us have such faith as will cause us to know that You are our Father, and the bestower of every good and perfect gift, and that only we, ourselves, can prevent Your Love changing us from the mortal to the immortal. (James 1:17-18)

Let us never cease to realize that Your Love is waiting for each and all of us, and that when we come to You, in faith and earnest aspiration, Your Love will never be withheld from us. (Luke 11:13)

Keep us in the shadow of Your Love every hour and moment of our lives, and help us to overcome all temptations of the flesh, and the influence of the powers of the evil ones, which so constantly surround us and endeavour to turn our thoughts away from You to the pleasures and allurements of this world. (Matthew 6:13; James 1:13-15)

We thank You for Your Love and the privilege of receiving it, and we believe that You are our Father — the loving Father who smiles upon us in our weakness, and is always ready to help us and take us into Your arms of Love. (Luke 15:11-32)

We pray this with all the earnestness and longings of our souls, and trusting in Your Love, give You all the glory and honour and love that our finite souls can give. Amen. (1 Timothy 1:17)

Prayers for Divine Love in the Bible

The New Testament contains several prayers for the Divine Love and related gifts:

Ephesians 1:16-19 – I have not stopped giving thanks for you, remembering you in my prayers. I keep asking that the God of our Lord Jesus Christ, the glorious Father, may give you the Spirit of wisdom and revelation, so that you may know him better. I pray also that the eyes of your heart may be enlightened *[prayer for better soul perceptions]* in order that you may know the hope to which he has called you, the riches of his glorious inheritance *[Celestial Kingdom]* in the saints, and his incomparably great power *[Divine Love that transforms our souls from divine image to divine substance and mortal to immortal]* for us who believe. That power is like the working of his mighty strength, ...

Ephesians 3:16-21 – I pray that out of his glorious riches he may strengthen you with power through his Spirit in your inner being, *[soul growth and soul perceptions through Divine Love]* so that Christ *[Divine Love]* may dwell in your hearts through faith *[Divine Love in the soul]*. And I pray that you, being rooted and established in love, may have power, together with all the saints, to grasp how wide and long and high and deep is the love of Christ, and to know this love that surpasses knowledge – that you may be filled to the measure of all the fullness of God. *[all Divine Love here]*. Now to him who is able to do immeasurably more than all we ask or imagine, according to his power that is at work within us *[this is awesome!]*, to him be glory in the church and in Christ Jesus throughout all generations, for ever and ever! Amen.

Philippians 1:9-11 – And this is my prayer: that your love may abound more and more in knowledge and depth of insight, *[prayer for growth in Divine Love and soul perceptions]* so that you may be able to discern what is best and may be pure and blameless until the day of Christ, filled with the fruit of righteousness that comes through Jesus

Christ – to the glory and praise of God. [*righteousness through soul-transforming Divine Love.*]

Colossians 1:3-6, 9-14 – We always thank God, the Father of our Lord Jesus Christ, when we pray for you, because we have heard of your faith in Christ Jesus and of the love you have for all the saints – the faith and love that spring from the hope that is stored up for you in heaven [*again, Divine Love*] and that you have already heard about in the word of truth, the gospel that has come to you. All over the world this gospel is bearing fruit and growing, just as it has been doing among you since the day you heard it and understood God's grace in all its truth. [*Divine Love is a gift of grace*]

Verses 9-14 – For this reason, since the day we heard about you, we have not stopped praying for you and asking God to fill you with the knowledge of his will through all spiritual wisdom and understanding *[soul perceptions]*. And we pray this in order that you may live a life worthy of the Lord and may please him in every way: bearing fruit in every good work, growing in the knowledge of God, being strengthened with all power according to his glorious might so that you may have great endurance and patience, and joyfully giving thanks to the Father, who has qualified you to share in the inheritance of the saints in the kingdom of light *[Celestial Kingdom reached through Divine Love]*. For he has rescued us from the dominion of darkness and brought us into the kingdom of the Son he loves, *[Celestial Kingdom of which Jesus is the Master]* in whom we have redemption, the forgiveness of sins *[through praying for and receiving the Divine Love]*.

Power of Soulful Longings

As mentioned, the above prayers give ideas how to ask for the Divine Love. But the Father will respond to every heartfelt prayer, as well as soulful, even unconscious longings. We'll conclude with a few thoughts from St. John to James Padgett (TGRABJ/2/185, paraphrased):

I heard your prayer and know that this Love is flowing into your soul and that you now have a great abundance of it. It will never fail you when you pray for it in earnestness and with real longings. It is always ready to respond to your aspirations. Have faith, and you will have the certainty of the Love seeking to come into your soul.

You are blessed to know of the existence of this Love, and that it may be yours if you desire it and pray with true longings of your soul. If you keep the consciousness of the presence of this Love continually alive, pray whenever the opportunity presents itself – even just moments when the mind may be free from business affairs – the longings, if exercised for only a moment, will bring results, for God's ear is always open and ready to respond.

Epilogue

This book has presented a fresh, non-traditional look at the Bible and Christian orthodox teachings. If the concepts presented here resonate with you and make sense, you have an exciting spiritual journey before you and a glorious destiny to work toward.

Adherents to all major religious traditions seek to find meaning to their life, both here and beyond. Most acknowledge the existence of a Higher Power as they understand it, such as the Source of all that is. Divine Love, the essence of a loving Creator God that He offers to share with humans if they wish to receive it, transcends all religions. If these teachings are true, they can be seen as a transcendent religion and a universal way to God and salvation (as opposed to the traditional belief that people have to become Christians and accept Jesus' sacrifice as a payment for their sins before they can be saved).

In a way, the overarching teaching of the availability of the Divine Love as a means for reaching a state of at-onement with God can be integrated into other religions. Believers of various persuasions, who already strive for a life of love, morality and ethics can adopt the concept and through earnest prayer, have their souls transformed by the Divine Love. If and when this happens, their very partial understanding of the ultimate reality (which we all have) will also gradually grow.

Epilogue

People of different faiths hope and believe that this life is not all there is. If that's the case, it behoves all of us to gain more understanding of the next life and prepare for it here and now. I believe that seeking and growing in the Divine Love is the best answer. However, each person has to decide for themselves.

Ideally, humans need to ponder these important truths in this life as the spirit world will not greatly help them of and by itself to obtain a more enlightened insight. A spirit is only a human without a physical body and the accompanying cares of earthly life. Some, however, retain these cares for a long time after coming to the spirit world and are only relieved of them by paying the penalties of a violated law. By contrast, those spirits who resist the temptations to indulge their previous life passions and appetites are able to turn their thoughts to higher things and may soon realize that only the New Birth brought about by soul transformation through the Divine Love of the Father can help them reach their highest potential. This is a glorious destiny as immortal divine angels in the Celestial Kingdom of God of unlimited joy, beauty and happiness.

If you are ready to test the truth of the message in this book, why not commit to personally start praying for the Divine Love? Use the prayer following Chapter 12, or ideas from it or the biblical prayers that resonate with you, or simply your own sincere and heartfelt prayer. In a few weeks of earnest and consistent prayer, you are likely to

Epilogue

notice greater peace and closeness to the Creator, as well as more love, joy, happiness and serenity.

As you continue praying, your life will become more loving and less stressed. You'll grow in understanding of vital truths. And when your time comes to leave this world and enter the spirit world, you will be well on the way to the Celestial Kingdom of God that Jesus spoke about where unsurpassed bliss and happiness await those who have achieved at-onement with their Heavenly Father through soul transformation from divine image into divine substance by the Divine Love.

References

Books

True Gospel Revealed Anew by Jesus, Volumes 1-4 (Publisher: Foundation Church of the New Birth)

Angelic Revelations of Divine Truth, Volumes 1-2 (Publisher: Foundation Church of Divine Truth)

New Testament Revelations of Jesus of Nazareth (Publisher: Foundation Church of Divine Truth)

53 New Testament Revelations (Publisher: Foundation Church of the New Birth)

76 Sermons of the Old Testament of the Bible, by Jesus of Nazareth (Publisher: Foundation Church of the New Birth)

Websites

http://new-birth.net/

http://universal-spirituality.net

See also: http://universal-spirituality.net/wp-content/uploads/2014/10/Divine-Love-Resource-Guide-1-2017.pdf

Specific References

http://www.umc.org/what-we-believe/our-wesleyan-heritage (John Wesley)

https://new-birth.net/topical-subjects/reconciling-the-padgett-messages-to-the-bible/ (Mark Kramer)

https://www.jba.gr/Articles/jbafeb07.htm (Anastasios Kioulachoglou)

http://www.fcdt.org/messages/messages_toc.htm (David Lampron)

http://www.spiritualwarfareschool.com/library/Kenneth%20Hagin/The%20New%20Birth,%20Kenneth%20Hagin,%2040pg.pdf (Kenneth E. Hagin)

About the Author

Eva Peck has a Christian and international background. Through Christian work and teaching English as a foreign language in several countries, she has experienced a range of cultures, customs and environments. Having lived and worked in Australia, the United States, Europe, Asia, and the Middle East, she now draws on those experiences in her writing.

Eva refers to biblical passages in this book the way she has come to understand them. Having had the opportunity to fellowship with Christians from a variety of faith traditions, she also recognizes that many faith-related issues can be understood in more than one way.

Eva studied biological sciences as well as theology at the tertiary level and has a Bachelor's degree in Science and a Master's degree in Theology. She is also an ordained minister in the Foundation Church of Divine Truth. She lives in Brisbane, Australia, with her husband, Alex.

About the Author

The Pecks' co-authored books of spiritual nature include *Pathway to Life – through the Holy Scriptures* and *Journey to the Divine Within – through Silence, Stillness and Simplicity*. Both publications, as well as Eva's trilogy *Divine Reflections* and her other books can be ordered through Pathway Publishing. Most of these books are linked to Amazon and available also at other online outlets worldwide. Many can be downloaded for free as PDFs offered as service to those who are interested and to help them on their spiritual journey.

For more information about Pathway Publishing, www.pathway-publishing.org see the following pages.

About Pathway Publishing

Pathway Publishing is dedicated to sharing truth and beauty by publishing books that present what is true to life and reality, as well as what is lovely and inspirational. The goal is to not only provide sound information, but also to lift the human spirit.

Pathway Publishing has a vision of helping readers on their path of enlightenment and spiritual transformation. The wisdom and experience of spiritual teachers, thinkers and visionary writers from various backgrounds and faith traditions are recognized and valued.

Books produced by Pathway Publishing include books of spiritual nature, as well as books featuring the art, photography and Czech poetry of Eva's father, Jindrich (Henry) Degen, now in his mid-nineties, but still very creative and productive.

- *Divine Reflections in Times and Seasons,* Eva Peck (2013)
- *Divine Reflections in Natural Phenomena,* Eva Peck (2013)
- *Divine Reflections in Living Things,* Eva Peck (2013)
- *Divine Insights from Human Life,* Eva Peck (2013)
- *Pathway to Life - Through the Holy Scriptures,* Eva and Alexander Peck (2011)

About Pathway Publishing

- *Journey to the Divine Within – Through Silence, Stillness and Simplicity,* Alex and Eva Peck (2011)
- *Jesus' Gospel of God's Love,* Eva Peck (2015)
- *Abundant Living on Low Income,* Eva Peck (2016)
- *The Greatest Love,* Eva Peck (2016)
- *Salvation,* Eva Peck (2017)
- *New Birth – Pathway to the Kingdom of God,* Eva Peck (2017)
- *Artistic Inspirations - Paintings of Jindrich Degen,* arranged by Eva and Alexander Peck (2011)
- *Colour and Contrast: Artwork of Jindrich Degen,* arranged by Eva and Alexander Peck (2013)
- *Faces and Forms Across Time: Artwork of Jindrich Degen,* arranged by Eva and Alex Peck (2013)
- *Variations: Art Exhibitions of Jindrich Degen,* arranged by Eva and Alex Peck (2013)
- *Nature in Art: Artwork of Jindrich Degen,* arranged by Eva and Alex Peck (2014)
- *Spirituality in Art: Artwork of Jindrich Degen,* arranged by Eva and Alex Peck (2014)
- *Floral and Nature Art – Photography of Jindrich Degen,* arranged by Eva and Alexander Peck (2011)
- *Nature's Beauty: Art Photography of Jindrich Degen,* arranged by Eva and Alex Peck (2013)
- *Verše pro dnešní dobu (Contemporary Verse), Jindrich* Degen (in Czech) (2011)

About Pathway Publishing

- *Volné verse* (Free Verse), Jindrich Degen (in Czech) (2012)

Some of the publications are also available as e-books. Many are downloadable for free as PDFs as a service to God's children worldwide. (See: http://universal-spirituality.net/home-2/free-publications)

Pathway Publishing

Seeking truth and beauty

www.ingramcontent.com/pod-product-compliance
Lightning Source LLC
Chambersburg PA
CBHW050552300426
44112CB00013B/1891